KU-603-880

WOMEN ON RAPE

JANE DOWDESWELL

FOREWORD BY ANNA RAEBURN

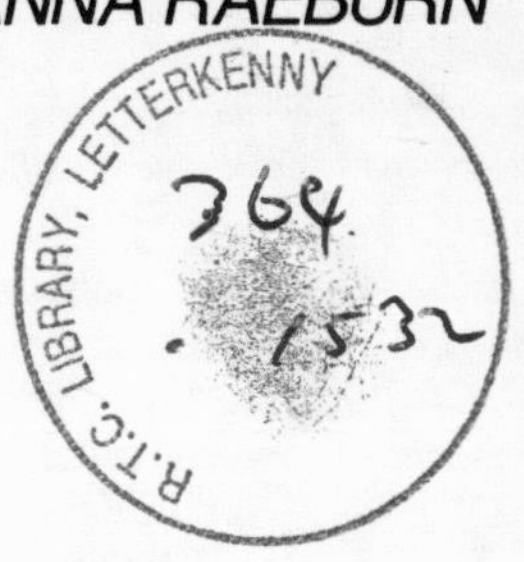

First published 1986

British Library Cataloguing in Publication Data

Dowdeswell, Jane
Women on rape
1. Rape, Britain
I. Title II. Series
364.1'532'0942 HV6569.G7

ISBN 0-7225-1213-9

Grapevine is an imprint of the Thorsons Publishing Group, Wellingborough, Northamptonshire, NN8 2RQ, England.

Printed in Great Britain by
Biddles Limited, Guildford, Surrey

3 5 7 9 10 8 6 4 2

Dedication

To Mum and Dad for your constant support and to Maggie for all your encouragement.

Contents

Foreword

This book is going to make you feel very sick and very angry. The public image of rape, even among the sympathetic, is that of an attack upon the vagina of a woman by an assailant or assailants unknown. The reality is that more than half the time, the assailants are known. Some of them may be well known, like your husband, your boyfriend, a colleague from work or your father. And the attack is upon your whole person. You can be harassed and humiliated and violated through every orifice. What is so often not taken into consideration is the psychological experience – the feeling of fear and powerlessness.

The idea that if you don't make a fuss you won't get hurt is set firmly to one side, thank heaven. Know that you may get hurt and be prepared to fight back if you can because it will help to maintain your feelings of self worth in the face of your humiliation and distress. Learning to fight back is less to do with prowess at unarmed combat than a willingness to acknowledge that you are right to fight.

This book also makes clear that the law as it stands in this country is not as imperfect as the interpretation of that law and underlines again that until rape is considered as a crime of violence, it will never be taken as seriously as it should be.

Every woman dreads rape. Some dwell on it to such an extent that they hate all men and thus – to them – all potential rapists. Others will not go out at night. Still more block it from their minds with the old charm, 'It can't happen to me.' But it happens to far too many women for us to ignore it, or to ignore how other people respond to it, whether family, friends or the professions from whom you might have to seek advice.

Women have just begun to open up on this subject and the point of this book is not to show you your experience duplicated within these pages, but rather that each person's experience is deeply personal and individualistic. What you can draw from the recounting of another person's experience is the courage to tell your own. For the telling of what happened to you is both the first step in your own mending and the first step to delineating your attacker.

This year the figures for rape have increased and the violence of the attacks has increased also. But if the official figures have gone up, it means that more people are prepared to bear witness about what happened to them. And this year several police forces put forward new initiatives designed to make breaking the silence easier.

Books about rape range from the passionate to the polemic. *Women on Rape* makes it clear that until we break the silence, our attackers break us. I hope you will read this book before you might need it.

ANNA RAEBURN

Introduction

My first conversation with a woman who had been raped made a lasting impression on me. It was many years ago now, when I was interviewing for a magazine article, but I remember it vividly. She came to the door of her flat and I heard several bolts being drawn back before it was opened narrowly, chains fastened. I can still see the frightened, distrustful eyes in a pale nervous face. She spoke almost in a whisper. She had been attacked two years before but to me it might have been yesterday.

At the time, I had thought her reaction extreme; now I know the only unusual part was that she was able to speak about her experience – thousands of women are probably suffering similarly but in silence. In fact, it has been shown that the way rape affects women is more severe than in the case of almost any other crime. One reason, perhaps, is that rape is a difficult subject to talk about. For the victim. For all of us.

When I first mentioned to people that I was writing a book, they were interested and wanted to know more. When told the subject was rape there was an uneasy silence from most, embarrassment from some, and a few tried to treat it as a joke – men in particular.

Not surprising then that women have found it difficult, if not impossible, to talk openly about rape. Instead, some have turned to newspaper or magazine articles, searching for women who have had similar experiences – but have found none. Or to books – but all they have found were statistics and the words of 'experts'. I was aware of a number of books written about rape and sexual abuse, but I hadn't really known that there was such a lack of real information on rape from the people it most concerns: women.

Reports from Rape Crisis Centres have gone a long way towards increasing our knowledge of reported and unreported rapes, yet even they cannot include *all* women, as many do not contact the police or Rape Crisis. The Women's Safety Survey, conducted by campaigning group, Women Against Rape, was the first large-scale survey about the incidence and the effects of rape and sexual assault, written, distributed and analysed by women, and as such began to show the reality of rape.

I hope this book will help fill the void by bringing together the words of women for others to read, to understand, and, perhaps, to identify with. Although I started my research with government reports, statistics, articles and papers – of which there are many – it was not until I began talking to women that I understood the depth of the trauma.

I appealed to them through personal columns and magazines. I was concerned they should not think I was exploiting their experiences, or that I would expose them – for this reason all names are changed in the book. I was warmed by their response – once we had made initial contact the bond between us became strong, even with women I have still never met face to face.

Some had never spoken to anyone before, some had. There were those who went through great anguish reliving the ordeal, yet most said it helped them to talk. *All* wanted to help other women by sharing their own experiences. As time went on, more women contacted me direct when they heard I was writing this book, and many people I spoke to knew other women who had also been raped. The official statistics seemed somehow almost irrelevant as woman after woman spoke of her experiences – we can only hazard a guess at the number of silent women, everywhere.

This is a book written by one woman, but containing the words of many. Isolation adds to the suffering: this book puts you in touch with other women to find out what they have been through, how they felt, and perhaps gain something from their words. The words of women who have been raped or sexually assaulted. Women who are angry at how the fear of rape restricts them. Women who are more afraid of rape and sexual assault than any other crime. Women who care enough to want to be involved and to change the attitudes which still prevail in the Eighties. Attitudes that are largely based on ignorance.

Among the most powerful is the belief that rape is a sexual act when a woman doesn't want it. Women and men, of all ages, expressed this in different ways, and yet in most cases it is the violence which is the overriding thing: a man seeking power and control, not passion. Violence.

In these pages you can read the reality of rape. To give help to those who have never spoken and perhaps think their experiences singular to them; to show how other women have faced up to what has happened, and come to terms with it. The importance of family and friends cannot be overestimated, nor should *their* suffering be ignored as they can be the so-called 'hidden victims' – male partners or relatives in particular – who often find it hard to understand the depth of the trauma; who want to help, but do not know how.

It is difficult to write such a book without alienating men completely. Many men have said they feel ashamed when they hear about a woman being raped, others became defensive, some angry. Whatever the reaction, the more people who read this book the better, to break down some of the ignorance. Men cannot experience it in the same way as women, but they can be more understanding and provide better support if a woman close to them is raped.

Even now, I can still remember my own initial doubts about writing this book. Was I the right person? There was no personal experience, so how could I talk to all these women and say I understood how they felt? I was told it was probably better that way: I could be less impassioned, more objective. That thought was often in the back of my mind. It was well-meant, but meaningless. No woman can write about rape and be objective. Rape is an issue which affects all our lives.

However, I have let other women 'talk', for I feel it is their words which are important. Without these women there would not have been a book; my thanks are to all of them for taking the time and finding the strength to talk to me.

Rape has been a silent subject far too long. These women are helping to break the silence. Listen to what they have to say. . . .

1

THE ACT OF RAPE: A Crime of Violence

'I can remember thinking, this isn't happening to me. I was like a zombie. He dragged me on a refuse site and raped me. But it wasn't violent, like you read about. He was very gentle, more like "making love" to me. He was even kissing me, that's what really disgusted me. Afterwards he said, "You're a really nice girl. I wish I'd met you somewhere else." ' *Vanessa, 18, from London.*

'I thought everyone had secrets with their uncles. Sometimes he would make me touch him or other times he would say his "friend" wanted to come inside me as he was lonely. He was always very gentle with me, but he said if ever anyone found out I'd be taken away and put in a home. It went on for six years until he went abroad to work. It was only when I got older I realized what had happened to me. We're told to watch out for strangers, but you're brought up to trust and respect your family.'
Sarah, 25, from Manchester.

'After I'd been beaten the second time I couldn't feel anything any more. I'm no prude but even I could not have imagined some of the things they made me do. I could see the pleasure in their faces (faces I knew quite well) when they saw how disgusted I was, how ashamed I felt. I really thought I was going to die, and I wanted it to happen quickly. I did not know how badly I was hurt until they left me on the floor of my bedroom and I saw myself in a mirror. Then I wanted to die again. No-one tells you how bad it can be: you think it'll be the physical act, that you'll submit to save your life, you'll be upset for a few days and then you'll get over it.'
Deirdre, 39, from Oxford.

These three women had never spoken about rape before. All had wanted to talk about it and had searched through books and magazine articles, looking for women who had similar experiences or were feeling as they did, but all they found were statistics, and the words of 'experts'. They each felt theirs was not the 'stereotype' rape: the rape that happens in a dark alley where the rapist is a faceless monster dressed in black.

If you asked people to set a scene for the act of rape few would say their bedroom, tucked up under the duvet, watching Coronation Street. But it could be just as likely to happen in your own home as down some dark, deserted side street.

Most would describe the main character as swarthy, mad, uncontrollable. No-one tells you it could also be your boyfriend, your boss, your brother-in-law, or your father who rapes you. We are told to beware the maniac, the dark figure in raincoat who haunts dark alleys searching for targets on which to unleash his uncontrollable desires. As children, we are told it's dangerous to talk to strangers; and even knowing more about the true identity of many rapists as we get older, it is still difficult to throw off that early conditioning. Rape Crisis Centres around the country estimate that over half of all rapes are carried out by men known to their victim, from an acquaintance to a close friend or husband.

It is only in the last decade that many myths have been exploded, largely as a result of women talking about their own experiences. The Women's Safety Survey, carried out by the campaigning group Women Against Rape in 1984, was the first large-scale survey of its kind in this country, designed to find out about the incidence and effects of rape and sexual assault on women. It revealed that rape is a common – if largely silent and under-reported – crime in our society, and it is only by talking about it that we are beginning to find out the horrifying truth. It is well known that the official figures do not show the total amount of crimes committed. Evidence from the Women's Safety Survey found that one in six women had been raped, and nearly one in three sexually assaulted. Yet the official statistics show that over 1,500 women and girls were raped in Britain in 1984, a 50 per cent increase on ten years ago, but still way below the real number. In London alone 365 rapes were reported in 1984. Using these official statistics we could estimate that one rape a day is reported to police in the Metropolitan area alone, while in Britain it is more like one rape every six hours. Yet this is just the tip of the iceberg, and these figures should be multiplied perhaps ten or twenty times to get the truth.

What we can know for certain, however, is that women of all ages, from three to ninety-three can be victims of rape or sexual assault. A high number are under twenty-five, yet possibly these are the women most able to talk about their experience, either to the police, or to Rape Crisis Centres. In 1979, of those women who revealed their ages to LRCC, over fifty per cent were under twenty years of age, and in the Women's Safety Survey, of those who had been raped or sexually assaulted, nearly half said it had happened when they were fifteen or younger. Yet in the course of their existence Rape Crisis Centres have been contacted by, or on behalf of, women and girls of all ages, all classes and all races. Our very sex makes us victims; no woman is immune. As Women Against Rape once said, 'It is now perfectly clear that individual men rape individual women and girls in all kinds of circumstances.'

The known rapist

Contrary to the stereotype image of the stranger who strikes in a dark alleyway or churchyard, you are more likely to be raped by someone you know or have seen before the assault. Strangers are involved in less than half the number of attacks, and it is more likely to be a casual acquaintance, ex-boyfriends, friends, family or neighbours. Rapists can be husbands, lovers, fathers, employers, the boy next door, the delivery man, the man you work with:

> I thought I'd be able to spot a rapist a mile off. But somehow when a man is attractive, well dressed and so pleasant, it doesn't occur to you that he could rape you. It was our office party and I got talking to this bloke who'd been working with us for just a week. He seemed really nice: very friendly. I didn't fancy him or anything, and he was telling me about his wife; they'd been married for two years. Anyhow, it turned out he lived a couple of roads away from me, so he offered me a lift home. I wouldn't just accept a lift from anyone: I'm not stupid, but he seemed so nice. Instead of driving straight home, he took another route as he said he had to call in at a friend's house. He drove to the ring road round the airport,

stopped the car, and raped me. I don't remember much of what happened, I was so shocked. It was as though I'd been knocked out with chloroform. I thought of getting out of the car and running, but where to? I've not been to work since, and hardly go out in case I see him. Sometimes I remind myself that it wasn't me that did wrong. But when it's someone who's so pleasant you can't help thinking it was your own fault. *Sandra, 28, from Slough.*

Rapists can be 'nice' men too: women are not prepared for this and find it difficult to talk about it to anyone when the man concerned is well known and well-liked.

I'd been babysitting for Dave and Ann since I was fourteen. They both played for the local darts team and had a regular night out each week. He had always been my childhood dream: he used to tease me and joke around with me. They only lived next door and Ann was my mum's best friend. A year ago, Dave came home early one Tuesday without Ann: he said they'd had a row and she'd gone home with a friend. I said I'd go as I was feeling tired, I went to get up and he grabbed me by the hair. I didn't know what he was doing at first, it was as if he was mucking about with me. He pulled me up the stairs: I was so frightened I was making these little sobbing noises, trying to scream. I was on my hands and knees, trying to get away, but he was very strong. He tried to have sex with me, but couldn't do it, he got angry and started swearing at me saying I'd always led him on, teased him. He said if I ever said anything he'd tell Ann that I'd wanted him to do it, and that everyone would know that I was easy. I see him almost every day: sometimes if I'm in the garden I see him looking out of the window at me. I hate him more than I can say, but everyone else thinks he's wonderful. *Joanne, 19, from Lewisham.*

It is generally held that being raped by a man you know is less damaging and distressing to the victim, but through talking to women it is clear this is just another myth.

Jenny, a student from Brighton, was raped when she was eighteen by the person she most trusted:

My rapist wasn't the violent stranger most people imagine rapists are. This was my boyfriend. I was doing 'A' levels, intending to study for a degree and aiming for a good career. The last thing I wanted was a baby. I had a physical relationship with him in which

> I enjoyed him entering my vagina with his hand. He knew this was as intimate as I was prepared to be.
>
> Unfortunately, this made rape very easy for him. He simply swopped his hand for his penis. I did not consent, I did not even realize what was happening. I did sense a change in his movements and was afraid of what this meant, but I was numb. In my confusion I was absolutely silent. He confirmed my fear immediately afterwards by apologising. I can remember thinking 'This is Rape'; he looked like a stranger all of a sudden, but he was looking at me with concern and feeling in his eyes. No, he couldn't be a rapist, but then why did I feel so cold? Subtle seduction or subtle rape? I believe the latter.

Questioning ourselves about whether it is rape, reveals our own confusion. Julie from Northampton would agree:

> I always used to think that girls and women were raped or attacked by strangers, but I knew the boy who raped me. I was walking home with a friend at night, and on the opposite side of the road we saw a lad we knew: he had been out with one of my friends from school. We called over hello, and he came over. I thought he was drunk because he had a glass in his hand – it was Whit weekend and people were taking their glasses around with them from pub to pub. He held the glass and smashed it against the wall, holding it close to my face, and said, 'Shut up, or you'll get this.' I laughed, as I thought he was joking, but he pushed me into a garden. My friend ran off as she said she was scared, and I was screaming and had cut my hand. He was lying on top of me and I remember trying to get up and seeing my legs under his body so I couldn't move. He held me down half-way between my chest and neck, and pulled my knickers down. I just kept screaming and eventually he ran off. I had marks on my thighs for weeks after, and when I got home my face and legs were streaked with blood – I think he'd cut himself on the glass. I've not told my mum or anyone else about it, as I think a lot of people wouldn't believe me and would think I encouraged him.

Often the rape or assault seems unreal even to you. At first you may find it difficult to see it as 'rape', particularly if the man involved is known to you. In an attempt to survive, mentally, some women tell how they tried to convince themselves it wasn't really happening to them.

Sandra was raped by a man who was given her address by a friend:

> She was chatted up by this South African guy we met at a nightclub and because of some instinct or something, she tried to get rid of him, so she gave him a false name and address (mine!). The next day, Sunday, at about 9 a.m. the doorbell rang and this guy was standing there. I recognized him, and he became very angry and said my friend had been playing games with him and he didn't like it. He just pushed his way into the house and threw me down on to the hall floor, then dragged me into the living room. I had slept with a man before the rape, my second boyfriend, and I tried to think that this was what I had done with my boyfriend and tried to blank out the fact that this man was not someone I cared for. I just knew instinctively there was nothing I could do to dissuade him, and in a way I just went off into a sort of a trance. It was like going out of your body, trying to dissassociate myself from what was happening to me. I felt like I was in a time warp – while I could keep myself in this cocoon where it was all unreal, I'd be able to survive whatever he did to me!

This 'blocking out' of everything around them is not uncommon says Dr Gillian Mezey from the Institute of Psychiatry, who has spoken to many rape victims in the course of her research. She says: 'There is often a narrowing of perception that occurs during attacks when women are not really aware of what is going on around them. One said, "All I could think about was the blue button, that blue button on the rapist's shirt". So while he was doing all these dreadful things, all the senses became narrowed down to this one single perception. I found this helps a lot of women get through it. Another woman remembers the area in the small of the back that was being rubbed up and down on concrete and the skin being grazed. She was just concentrating on that so much she couldn't remember anything else.'

Time and place

We are led to believe that rape occurs often in streets and dark alleys but the circumstances can be wide and varied. As examples, here are four very different settings. Read them through and decide which you think was the place and who the victim of a crime:

- 7 a.m. – a fourteen-year-old girl sets out on her paper-round in Sevenoaks. It's her regular route and she sees the same few joggers, and workers on their way to the station . . . .
- Noon – a pensioner leaves the busy shopping centre, already crowded with shoppers, calls into Woolworth's and the Post Office to collect her pension . . . .
- 3 p.m. – a nurse on nightshift sleeps in the flat she shares with her friend, also a nurse, who is getting ready to leave for work . . . .
- Midnight – two girls walking home after a night at the local club. They stop at the bus shelter to check on the last buses. A car pulls up – it's the father of one of their friends – and offers them a lift. They are relieved: it was going to be a long walk home.

The frightening answer is that each setting we've described was witness to rape. No better proof, if it is needed, that rape can happen *anywhere,* to *any one* of us at *any time*.

Behind closed doors

According to the Women's Safety Survey, the *most* common place that rape occurs is in the home: nearly a third of those women who had been raped or sexually assaulted said that it had happened in their own home. This is where all the myths are blown: most women may feel frightened on the streets, but once home, feel safe. Here your defences are down – you are at your most vulnerable.

Take one woman's story: It was 1 am, on 12 January 1982. Julie had switched off the television after watching the late night movie. It was like any other night, except she was alone – her friend had gone to stay with her boyfriend in Southampton. Julie was going into work late next day so she thought she'd take a book up to bed and read for a while. She remembers the next twenty-four hours as though it was yesterday:

There was a knock at the door, and at first I thought it was Sue, that perhaps she'd decided not to go to Dave's house after all. I had a chain on the door as I opened it but when I saw it was Jonathan, Sue's younger brother, I took it off. I'd met him at a party a couple of months before, for their parents' anniversary. I was a bit surprised to see him but I invited him in and made us some coffee. He told me he was up in London for some job interviews, had gone for a few drinks with some friends and missed the last train home. I said he could sleep in Sue's room as she was away.

I woke in the night feeling as though I couldn't breathe. He was sitting astride my chest, completely naked and tried to force his penis into my mouth. I'd always maintained I'd fight like hell if someone tried to rape me. I'm a nurse so I'm used to lifting patients, but I couldn't move. I tried to struggle, to turn my head but he said, 'If you keep on, you're going to end up getting cut' – he had a pair of scissors in his hand. He subjected me to all kinds of abuse, verbal and physical. I tried to talk him round, say I'd always fancied him, but he accused me of treating him like a child, as though he was stupid. He slapped me round the face – he wanted me to respond, to fight him, but I know when I'm beaten. After doing all kinds of things, some you could not even imagine and which I cannot even now talk about, he started kissing me, and that made me feel sick: I really thought I was going to throw up. After being so violent, he suddenly turned 'caring' – that's not the right word but I don't know how else to describe it. He said he'd always wanted me, and when I'd left my bedroom door open – which I always do from habit – he knew I wanted him too. I couldn't believe what I was hearing: he said he'd move to London and we could get a flat together! I just told him to get out, to never come near me again.

I've never spoken about it to anyone, not even Sue. She is probably the last person I'd have said anything to, but it ruined our friendship anyway and I moved into my own flat. I wish sometimes I'd reported him, but the way he was afterwards made me feel I was partly to blame. It wasn't as though I'd been attacked walking home from the hospital by someone I'd never seen before – perhaps in a way I'd have been more prepared for that.

On the streets

Our awareness is greater when walking along dark streets and alleyways, through deserted car parks, and shopping centres, at night, and waiting for buses and trains. Here the fear is of the stranger-rapist – research has shown that of those women who are raped or sexually assaulted, more than a quarter are assaulted in a street or alleyway.

From the information available it does also seem most rapes occur in the night hours, perhaps when women are trying to get home from a night out, or working late and all the last buses and trains have long gone. Yet it could be just as likely on your way home from work in the early evening.

Vanessa, 18, says:

> I'd gone late-night shopping after work. I had a job in the City as a secretary and was staying with my gran in Mitcham. It was a February night, about eight o'clock, on a Tuesday, so it was quite dark, but you'd think that at eight o'clock you'd be perfectly safe. You just don't expect it to happen to you and I wasn't on my guard. I'd got off the bus and was walking down the road to my Nan's flats. I'd been there so many times. I heard these running footsteps behind me as I approached the lift, but it didn't really register. I thought it was someone who had seen me getting the lift and was running to catch it, because you wait ages once you've missed one. I had just pressed the button, when this man suddenly appeared and pounced. I froze and he said, 'Shut up, don't make a noise.' I remember thinking this isn't happening to me. He dragged me to this refuse site around the back of the flats. He wasn't rough with me when he raped me, in fact he was quite gentle. I was just in a zombie state, I don't know how long it lasted, it could have been two minutes, it could have been two hours. In a way it seemed to go on for ever. It wasn't violent, like the kind you read about, it was like he was actually making love to me; he was kissing me so intimately, that's what I found disgusting. He even started talking to me afterwards – that really freaked me out. He asked me if I had a boy friend and I said I had and he told me not to tell him or anyone about what had happened. He got up and dressed and then as he went to leave he said, 'You're a really nice girl, I wish I'd met you somewhere else.' I was just sitting there in total shock. – Great! Rape me and then tell me that!

Even being aware of the risks is not enough. Sally's father always picked her up at the shop where she worked after school. But it was a few days before Christmas and she got off early:

> I tried to ring him but as it was only eight o'clock I thought I'd be okay to walk home on my own. I am aware of risks and dangers, in fact, there's a subway nearby and I waited to walk through with other people so I wouldn't be on my own. I always look behind me too, but it was a very well-lit road and quite busy. When I got to the corner I met a friend and we were talking and saw this boy watching us. We didn't really think about it, apart from having a bit of a joke and said he was probably waiting to jump on one of us, you know, like you do when you're mucking around. She left me and I walked on. I was literally five minutes from my house when I heard something behind me. I thought, I'm not going to let anyone scare me, so I turned round sharply to face them. I nearly died – I saw this boy literally crawling along the floor behind me, stalking me like an animal. I'll never forget seeing him like that. Before I could turn and run he'd jumped on my back and dragged me down. I couldn't scream at first as he had his hand over my mouth and as he'd grabbed me I was winded anyway. He pushed me against the fence and as I fell to the floor I tried to scream. I'd heard people say they couldn't scream, but you know, I could actually feel the muscles in my throat seizing up. All I could do was grab my shoe and I just started bashing him on the head. He'd pushed me to the floor and I couldn't get up – it was really frosty and slippery. He stuck his hand up me, but I started to scream and eventually he got up, looked round and ran off. As soon as he ran off I really found my voice and started screaming. The neighbours said they'd heard my first screams. It happened right against the garden wall, so they must have heard something, but they said they thought it was someone mucking about.

The fact is, you can't rely on other people when you're being attacked, and you have only to look in the newspapers to see that is true:

One report told of a terrified student who was being chased by a rapist and so grabbed a passer-by's arm and begged him to help. He looked the other way and told her to 'clear off'. The attacker, posing as her boyfriend, dragged her away, and viciously beat her up before raping her.

A young woman who was sexually assaulted in a London tube station on a Saturday afternoon said, 'What haunts me most is that hundreds of people walked past, ignoring my screams. One man actually shook me off when I grabbed his legs and pleaded for help.'

An eighteen-year-old student on her way home after an evening class studying for 'A' levels, was dragged along a busy street in Brixton, yet passers-by ignored her screams. She says, 'I was shouting and telling him to let go of my arm. One woman just turned round and walked the other way. He dragged me past a bus queue, and they all just stared and did nothing.' She was taken to a squat, and when she refused to undress he pulled a knife and raped her.

Perhaps, then, it's not surprising that we know so little of what goes on behind closed doors.

Within the family

Rape within marriage is still dismissed as something that doesn't really happen, and in law it *doesn't* exist. Yet the Women's Safety Survey by Women Against Rape discovered that one in seven of married women had been raped by their own husbands. For women who are, or have been married, the WSS found it is more common than any other rape. This is backed up with other research. In New South Wales, a magazine survey found that thirteen per cent of all women who had been raped, had been raped by their husbands and in San Francisco there have been similar statistics. This means that even in the shortest London street there must be several homes which have a history of rape, or in which rape is still part of married life. Like incest and battered wives, rape in marriage is another taboo subject. Wife battering was hidden away until brought to public attention in the seventies with the opening of refuges. The number of women who fled to them showed that there was a hidden demand by women desperate to escape violent husbands and boyfriends. Until then – and still now – it happened behind closed doors, but once you look inside, the more you find.

Sexual abuse can often go on for long periods of time: the women usually have no other place to go; their financial dependence makes them vulnerable to rape. Some women who have been forced to give into sex against their will in marriage do *not* consider it rape. They see it as their duty. 'It is only now that I realize it was not normal for a husband to force his wife to have sex. I'm old-fashioned too – I believe it's my duty to cook and clean, but even I draw the line now at being a sexual slave.'

Some had experienced physical violence, or threats that the 'housekeeping' money would be stopped or that the children would suffer. Children are often the reason women stay and as soon as the children left home they felt more able to find a place of their own:

> I used to submit when our two children were home; he was very violent and I was afraid for them too. But now they've both left home, I just walked out. I'd have liked to tell people why I left, but who believes you? All our friends are his friends too, even my parents who are now elderly think the world of him. It was enough to tell them I was leaving, but to tell them what had happened, well I don't know what their reaction would have been.
>
> *Mary, 50, from Newcastle.*

The threats used are often cruel and effective:

> He used to come home every Friday night, as 'drunk as a lord'. I'd always make sure we were all in bed, put the children in their rooms and lock the doors. Then I'd pretend to be asleep, but he would wake me up demanding I be a 'proper' wife to him. He would threaten me, that he'd wake the children and see what they thought of their mother, that he would forbid me to have my friends or my parents round. He didn't threaten me with violence, but I always felt terrified: if I made one wrong move I'm sure he would have beaten me. *Joan, 32, from Cardiff.*

Non-physical threats are common-place where the rapist knows the woman. One woman said she could not report being raped by her boss as he threatened her with dismissal and as a single mother with a young baby she had already had great difficulty in finding a job and somewhere to live.

This is also true where it involves young girls: emotional blackmail, coercion, and the position of authority are all used, particularly where the man is someone who has been given specific authority over children – such as a babysitter or a teacher – and where the child is raped or sexually assaulted by someone in their family.

Suffer little children

More girls are abused than boys, and the majority of abusers are male. Although young girls are raped by 'strangers', the majority of rapes are by people known to them, either casual acquaintances, or with people they have day-to-day contact like school friends and relatives and, as we've said, particularly by those in a position of authority and trust over them including fathers, grandfathers, brothers and uncles. When it is rape within blood relatives, it is usually classed as incest, and using this phrase often conceals rape. The word 'incest' suggests consent, yet most young girls are not in a position to agree or oppose. Very often they do not know what 'sex' is, and are searching for love and affection, so can get this confused with other shows of attention.

Carole, from Hampshire, was just eleven when her uncle started making sexual advances towards her:

> At the time my parents were newly divorced and I turned to my favourite 'auntie', who I think the world of, for comfort. My uncle used to offer to take me home in his car, call round to visit me whilst my father was working – I lived alone with my father at that time – and generally take advantage of every opportunity to be alone with me.
>
> He would sometimes put his arms around me, kiss me goodbye, ask me to take my heavy school jumper off and to sit next to him. He said it would be our secret, because if my father knew he might be jealous and we might upset him, so for his sake it was best if we said nothing. I thought of him as a father figure in a way, and no thought of perversion occurred to me at that age; they just seemed like innocent, loving gestures. I desperately needed to feel loved and wanted at that time.
>
> For three years I went through heavy petting, sexual abuse, livid language, pornographic literature and near rape. My younger cousin chose that moment to burst into the kitchen, thank God. It was only later that I realized what he had been doing to me, but I did not confide in anyone, despite my father gently coaxing me to talk to him as to my sudden withdrawn moods. How do you put into words what is happening to you, when you're too young to really understand what is going on and think adults know what is right?

As children, we are brought up to trust adults and not to challenge what they say. Violence and force are not needed, as children respond in the way they are told to, they think it is what is expected. One young girl was continually assaulted by her grandfather when she sat with him in the back seat of the family car (her parents were in the front). She never said a word, until eventually it was discovered and she said she had thought it was what all grandfathers did to their grandchildren. A child will go along with it, as she thinks it is right, and this makes it easier for the attacker to blame the child and find excuses for his behaviour. It can also make the victim feel guilty in time, and even less likely to say anything about what is happening.

Louise was raped by her father from the age of seven to when she was sixteen. It started with threats and continued because she felt guilty and unable to tell anyone:

> My nightmare began when my father locked my mother in the bathroom after they had been fighting. I went down to plead with him to let her out. He said he'd only let her out if I did certain things and allowed him to do things to me. This was the beginning, from simple petting to oral sex and actual intercourse. I agreed that first time in order to save my mother, and by doing so I had consented to what went on between us. He didn't need to force me, or threaten me with violence, but his methods were much more cruel. I was told that if I told on him he'd kill my sister and my mother. I know now that it was an empty threat but at that age I totally believed in what he said, and I thought I was saving the lives of my family. It happened time and time again, eventually even when my mother was walking freely around the house.
>
> The most desperate stage in my life was when he tried to do the same things to my sister. Being the eldest, I felt it was my duty to protect her. I placed squeaky toys around her bed at night so in the dark he would be unable to avoid stepping on them. I rushed in and, in a desperate attempt to save my sister, offered myself to him instead. This now transferred the guilt to me, as I'd 'asked' him to do these things to me, and he took advantage of this new situation and his visits increased from that time onwards.

Sexual abuse of this kind can be an isolated incident, but it often goes on for many years, undetected. The attacker relies on his victim's ability to keep quiet, and treat it as their little secret, as though it is some kind of new game, or by trading sweets and toys in return for secret cuddles and other little favours.

It's not surprising, then, that cases of rape within families, or by adults in a position of trust, rarely come to light. Some people still think if you ignore it it will go away. Or that it doesn't happen at all. Yet Rape Crisis Centres have been in touch with thousands of women and girls who have been raped by members of their family.

In Britain a MORI survey in November 1984 indicated that twelve per cent of women and eight per cent of men had been sexually abused before the age of sixteen, so, of the children in Britain today, over one million are likely to be sexually abused before the age of sixteen, and of those, they estimate, 143,000 of them by members of their family. There are no officially reliable statistics for the incidence of incest in England and Wales. However, a survey in *'19'* magazine in 1983, to which over 3,000 women responded, estimated that over one third were sexually abused as children, and half of those were incestuous cases. The Women's Safety Survey backs this up: one in five of their survey respondents remembered being raped or sexually assaulted as children or teenagers, and many by someone known to them.

Yet only about 300 cases of incest a year have been brought to the notice of the police in recent years.

Planned attack

Many men who rape, particularly those who rape young children known to them, plan in advance what they are going to do, and then carry out the plan when the opportunity arises: for example, when alone in the house with the child. This refutes the idea that rapists all attack at random when they are overcome by sudden uncontrollable sexual urges or desires.

One man spent a week setting up an elaborate attack. He approached an estate agents and asked for the keys to a vacant premises for sale. When the keys were returned one was found to be missing, but they had no way of contacting the man. A week later he waited outside a job centre in Birmingham, and approached a seventeen-year-old girl as she came out. He looked smartly dressed, middle-aged, quite respectable, and told her he was just about to place an advertisement for staff and suggested she call to see him the next day. He gave her the address of the premises which was, of course, the same place for which he had the keys: an office above a shop. As soon as she walked in he grabbed her and threw her, face down, on the floor. Her hands were tied behind her back and she was raped.

Another man saw a card in a newsagent's window advertising a babysitter's services. He phoned and arranged to meet the girl. When they met they walked along talking, but when they reached open ground he attacked her, threatened her with a knife, raped her and robbed her of 30 pence.

Bev from Manchester believes her rapist had planned the attack, which happened seven years ago, for several months:

> I had lived with some friends in Oxford for the whole of the summer and several suspicious things had happened: punctures on my car, someone prowling around outside, and one night there was even a stepladder up to my bedroom window! The police had shown little interest, but even so, when I went back to stay for the weekend, I was sufficiently concerned to insist I had a different bedroom. Unfortunately, the only spare one was on the ground floor. I'd been out with my boyfriend and on returning home at two o'clock in the morning I had fallen straight to sleep. I awoke a couple of hours later with the moon shining brightly into my room. For some reason I felt strangely anxious and was just about to get up, when suddenly, and very slowly, the bedroom door opened. It was like one of those nightmares you have in childhood – the door opens and instead of someone you know, it is a hideous unknown figure. It was dressed all in black, with a mask over his head, and he came towards me with a knife in his hand – a knife from our kitchen, I later discovered. For the next forty-five minutes, or hour, or however long it took, I could only do his bidding. He didn't beat me up or say anything but all the time was the threat of the knife. It was an hour of 'living death'. He pushed me under the duvet and I thought that was it, he was going to kill me. I lay there gritting my teeth and waiting for the plunge of the knife, but minutes passed and still nothing had happened. I gradually pushed the cover off my head, hardly daring to open my eyes in case he was there. But he was gone.
>
> When the police caught him, it turned out he knew my name, phone number, had seen me at parties and had followed me on a number of occasions, just waiting for the best time.

British and American reports have both shown that about eighty per cent of rapes are wholly or partially planned in advance, and this is even higher where rapes are committed by more than one assailant, which again are quite commonplace. One in three trials at the Old Bailey involved two or more defendants, according to Szuszanna Adler, who sat in on rape trials over a period of three years; and the Rape Crisis Centres find that multiple assailants are involved in about one in five attacks.

> We'd been travelling abroad for months and were always very careful to the point of paranoia, but we let our guard drop a bit when we reached the Galapagos Islands which are so idyllic that you can't imagine anything going wrong. Of course, as two Western women in such a small community, we didn't go unnoticed. A man we'd met had said we could stay at his house as apparently he had heard some guys talking in town about us. We were suspicious of *him*! It turned out these four guys had been smoking dope all day and they turned up in the middle of the night and raped us. We knew three of them by sight – one of them was the cook on a fishing boat we'd spent time on and apparently they'd found out we were alone on the camp site. It's frightening to think how they'd actually sat round and planned it all.
>
> *Carol V.*

Melanie, 22, was living and working in Brussels when she was raped by three boys in November 1983.

> I'd been out for a drink with some friends and it was very late when I left them to walk back to my car, which was parked down a side street some distance away. As I walked towards the car I saw three youths leaning on it, and I was not quite sure what to do. My friends had gone, so I couldn't go back. I deliberately did not look at them, but reached out with my car keys for the door. One of them grabbed my arm and pushed me into the car door. I don't think they realized I was English until I started shouting at them to leave me alone.
>
> They began to laugh at me, imitating my accent. The guy who looked as if he was the leader sat on the front of the car and watched the other two. First of all they were just pushing me from one to the other, then the pushes became quite hard and they started to pull my hair and hit me quite hard. I fell down and they

> began to kick me, all the time they were laughing and talking to each other.
>
> The guy who was sitting on my car said something to them, and they stopped kicking me and just looked at me. I thought that it was all over, that they would just go away and leave me alone, but they didn't. They unzipped their jeans and started to pull my clothes off. I really couldn't move. I was frozen, physically paralysed, conscious of what was happening to me, but powerless to do anything about it. They raped me, and one of them ejaculated into my mouth. I just could not believe this was happening to me.
>
> I didn't realize how badly hurt I was until a friend rushed me to hospital. I had wounds to my head that needed stitches, I had two broken ribs, and needed 11 stitches to my thighs and vagina.

Her story illustrates a frightening new trend of the 'opportunist' rapist as he is called. She is convinced too that it was the violence that incited them, the feeling of power they had over her.

A crime of violence

Rape is too often seen as a sexual crime. If you went out on the streets and asked people about their views on rape, most would inevitably relate it straight to sex. That is true of female attitudes, not just male: many women say they, too, thought of the actual act of intercourse as being rape and never thought of the violence involved. Said one woman: 'I'd always heard that if you don't resist you don't get hurt; after all it's only sexual intercourse, so the best thing is to just lie there and take it.' But rape is not like that at all; for a start your body doesn't react as it does when you consent to sex, and some women have been hurt by penetration alone. It can also include other forms of assault, such as forcing objects into the vagina or anus: one girl had a bottle forced into her vagina and it was then smashed. She needed twenty-seven stitches. A woman who was attacked in Glasgow by four boys was slashed with a razor on her face and neck. Locks of hair were scalped from her head and bone-deep wounds made in her thighs. She was left in a pool of blood, naked from the waist down, and when she arrived at hospital she was barely alive.

When rapists attack elderly women or very young children the

motive is usually not primarily sexual. The feeling of power and control is often greater when an old woman, for example, is involved, who is unable to fight back. There can be little sexual satisfaction of the sort most people understand. There was a case of two young boys in their late teens who came across an old woman sleeping rough, carrying her belongings in a huge laundry bag. She was filthy dirty and smelt terrible. They both raped her.
The two women who talk here suffered particularly violent attacks. The purpose is not to shock — although inevitably it will — but to reveal the hidden side of rape:

> I know it's been said before, but I agree, rape is not primarily a sexual act, but an act of violence. I could have been *any* woman – he was out to get a woman to submit to his will rather than take pleasure in sex. He was always calm but there was an undercurrent of violence which was all the more dangerous and I strongly felt that he meant to kill me. He did not appear to be acting out of lust for sex, but rather out of lust for power. He was interested in my subjugation rather than his sexual pleasure.
>
> It was almost five years ago when I was returning from a New Year's Eve party. I had dropped off four friends en route and was within five minutes of home, when a car overtook my car and rounded the corner onto a long, dark stretch of road. By the time I caught up with this car, the driver had parked it half on, half off the verge and was standing in the road flagging me down. It was icy and I thought there'd been an accident. So I stopped – I'm a nurse so thought they might need help.
>
> I had an old car and couldn't lock the door. He came to the driver's side and before I could do anything he had jumped in on me and grabbed the car keys. He pushed me over to the passenger seat and drove off, stopping about half a mile away in a dark country lane that is rarely used. He parked so that the passenger side of the car was wedged next to a high bank so that I couldn't get out.
>
> He raped me for over an hour and committed other acts. I was shocked into a kind of mental paralysis and I was convinced he intended to kill me. He ordered me to take all my clothes off even though it was freezing. He didn't remove any of his clothes, merely pulled down his trousers, so I felt extremely vulnerable and defenceless.
>
> I was sitting on the front passenger seat and he forced himself

between my legs with my feet on the dashboard. He wanted me to move about but I didn't and so he forced himself into my anus several times over. He didn't ejaculate and got very annoyed and said that I had to make him by any means I could and he pushed my head right down into the back of the car and sat on my chest and began masturbating into my face. I found this the most humiliating aspect and covered my face. He pulled my hands away and made me look at him. He said he had a woman friend who lived nearby and he said he was going to take me there and they were going to do all kinds of things to me.

In the driver's mirror I saw the lights of a car reflected, but as he had his back to it he coudn't see. I waited until the car was almost level and then screamed and screamed. The car drove on a little way and then stopped – he leapt out of the car and ran off. I don't know who the person in the other car was because I was so terrified in case he should come back, that somehow I managed to drive off as fast as I could. *Beth, from Sheffield.*

Another woman who has had the courage to talk about what happened to her while living and working in Australia, says:

I'd thought about the possibility of being raped. I think all women do, but you think of it being a physical attack, that you would give in for your life, and that you'd be upset for a few days, and then you'd get over it. I was totally unprepared when the guy attacked me and showed such total aggression against women. I really thought he was going to kill me.

Usually I'd have taken a cab home, but I'd had a bit of a row with my boyfriend and was feeling a bit unhappy, and so I decided to walk to give myself time to think. There were no cars about, apart from one which came from behind me and pulled up a little way in front. I was a little wary as there was no-one else about, so I crossed over but then he called out to me and started walking towards me. As this had happened a lot in London, I didn't run but just pretended I hadn't heard and carried on walking. The next thing I knew, someone spun me round and smashed me right in the face and I could feel instantly that all my front teeth had been pushed back into my mouth. In fact, I lost the whole lot.

I knew he meant business and that he would kill me. He dragged me into his car and drove to a deserted parking lot. I thought he was going to dump me somewhere.

He ordered me to take off my clothes, and when I didn't move he whacked me in the stomach. It's incredible that I didn't really panic at that point, I think you react differently when you know your life is at stake. I tried to say we could go back to my apartment instead. I thought if I could do that I might be able to escape. But it made him more angry, he said I was just trying to be clever, and hit me again. He raped me first in the car, then he ordered me to get out, and forced me to do so many violent and degrading acts. I'm pretty broad-minded, but what he did to me I could not even imagine.

He was inside my back passage for most of the time over a period of three hours – it was so painful. He put his fist up there too, and then forced his hand into my mouth – which was already bleeding – and when I went to wipe my lips I looked at my hand and it was brown where he had forced his hand so far inside me. It took days for that to go away.

He ordered me out of the car and dragged me down to some bushes where he went through the whole thing again. I tried to take my mind off the pain by trying to plan an escape. I couldn't believe it when he said he wanted to do the whole thing a third time. I begged him to let me go – I said I was going back to England and I wouldn't tell anybody, but he said he knew I'd go to the police, and I was sure he was going to kill me when he'd finished with me.

He was lying on the slope with his trousers round his ankles and was leading up to an orgasm. I could see he enjoyed the pain I was going through, the humiliation. There was a street light I could see up the hill through the trees, but I had to get up a steep embankment. There was this split second when I thought I had to try to run, he closed his eyes for a moment and I just ran and ran and never looked back. It's two years ago now, and yet I can still feel myself running. I knew I was running for my life and that pushed me on. It was the greatest fear I have ever experienced – to know you are so close to death. *Cathy, from London.*

The much-quoted phrase 'All men are potential rapists' should perhaps be re-written, said one woman, to read 'All rapists are potential murderers.' However, though most rapes do involve some physical force, few victims appear to sustain an injury requiring medical attention, and many rapists use the threat of violence rather than the actual act. There is no doubt, though, that the power is all important. Malcolm Fairley, the rapist the media called 'The Fox', described not the sexual satisfaction but the power: 'I felt like a king with the gun in my hand,' he said.

Fairley also illustrates another fact about rapists. It was because he was such a 'nonentity' that he evaded capture for so long. He had drifted from one casual job to another, making little impression or any friends. One acquaintance said of him: 'He was the sort of bloke you wouldn't notice in a crowd.' Researchers who have studied 'the rapist' have concluded that he is an 'ordinary man'. No great revelations there you might think, but important nevertheless, as people do tend to think you can spot a potential rapist a mile away. If all rapists were lunatics, wore dark macs and had shifty eyes, then indeed, that might be possible!

The newspaper headlines that call them 'sex beasts' or 'sex fiends' only add to the confusion by making us think of rape as an act committed by psychopathic monsters, maniacs out of control. In fact, very few rapists are referred for psychiatric treatment: in England and Wales less than two per cent of convicted rapists are referred for psychiatric treatment each year, which makes them just about the sanest prisoners around.

Most convicted rapists are young (many are under twenty-one) and see violence as a way of getting what they want. In *Why Men Rape*, a report by Sylvia Levine and Joseph Koenig (W. H. Allen), ten convicted rapists in Canada talk about their reasons. They talk of inadequacy, failing to live up to society's pressures to conform, their ignorance, their fears in forming relationships with people. Some think by having sex (even if it involves violence) they might find love. Some even try to be friendly after the rape, chatting to the woman, making her something to eat, offering to walk her home, as though rape is the start of a new relationship and the woman's fear a sign of friendship.

Contrary to the belief that men rape when overcome by strong sexual urges, and seek out any woman on whom to unleash them, most rapists are having regular sexual relationships at the time of the rape. However, in some cases the crime may follow an argument with another woman, and rape is used as an expression of hostility, or to prove their masculinity.

There is *nothing* absolutely certain about rapists apart from the fact that they are male.

Just as all women are possible 'targets' by the nature of our sex, so all men are capable of rape.

Men have a choice – most *choose* not to.

For women, rape is an act where there is no choice.

2
THE CRIME:
Attitudes and Law

'It's a well known fact that all women expect you to try something on. If you don't they think you're "queer" and if you take "no" for an answer they'll tell you you didn't try hard enough.'

Terry, 22, from Surrey.

'When I said "I do", I didn't know I was consenting in law to my husband's right to rape me. I didn't know the marriage certificate signed away a woman's rights to her own body.'

Jacqueline, 29, from Blackpool.

'I think there should have been Eleven Commandments – to include "Thou shalt not rape". Perhaps then the law would have taken it more seriously, and attitudes would be different. I feel very strongly that rape isn't about sex at all but about violence and power relations between men and women.'

Patricia, from South Wales.

If someone hits you over the head with an iron bar, or breaks into your home and steals your video, people don't ask if you've enjoyed the experience – of course they don't. But if you're raped people see it differently. Even though it can be a brutal crime, the sexual element takes over in people's minds, both male and female. It is perhaps the only crime where there is a general assumption that the victim might have 'enjoyed it'.

One woman who was raped said she could not believe the reaction of her next door neighbour: 'She actually told me that someone had asked her if it was she who had been raped, and she remarked "I should be so lucky!" She actually related this to me herself! I was unable to reply but clearly, she did not think she had said anything wrong.'

The assumption is that all women want to be raped: we fantasize about rape, so why wouldn't we enjoy it if it happened to us? But fantasy is quite a different thing to reality: in our fantasies it stops when we *want* it to stop, in rape there is no control. The notion that women say 'no' when they really mean 'yes' is also commonplace – even in the courtroom. A judge in his summing-up referred to the phrase, 'Stop it, I like it!'

There is the myth that rape is sex when the woman doesn't feel like it, or that rape is just 'over-energetic' intercourse. Again in court, rape has been referred to as 'making love'. There is no comparison: rape is not an act of love; rape is force, rape is brutal.

One teenage girl who was raped said the reaction of a male friend was: "I bet you enjoyed it once he got going. All girls like a bit of force." I couldn't believe it – I just exploded and said if someone beat him with a stick, humiliated him in the way I'd been, would he enjoy it? But it doesn't happen to a man like that, does it?'

Therein lies the root of the problem. Although men in general have become more sympathetic and understanding of many issues, they cannot experience rape in the same way as women – they cannot know the reality. The 'unknown' becomes something of a joke – it is easy to laugh about something you don't understand.

A young girl who was raped by 'The Fox', as he was known in the Press, said that if she mentions that she is from Edlesborough, boys have jokingly asked her if she was The Fox's victim. 'I usually answer in a matter-of-fact way, "yes, actually I was." They always become very sheepish.'

At the time of the Yorkshire Ripper (another media description), one girl walking along in Leeds was called to from a car by a group of young men. 'Are you looking for the Ripper?' they laughed.

It is also true that men joke about rape because they find it embarrassing or because they want to be 'one of the lads'. Making a joke out of rape isn't clever; it only shows ignorance. It is also a way of dismissing it: when a subject is 'too close to home' the easiest way out is to trivialize it. As one woman said, 'Men push the issue of rape away, shove the responsibility of rape off themselves so they don't feel any guilt.'

No wonder men don't blame themselves – the myth tells them

they have some primeval urge that once they see a woman dressed in a certain way they can't be responsible for the consequences: once aroused there is no return. Is this not an insult to the responsible male too?

Women are made to feel responsible for their own *and* men's sexuality. We're encouraged to make ourselves attractive, to wear make-up and fashionable clothes, while magazines feature articles on how to attract a boyfriend and how to increase your confidence with the opposite sex. All this is easily turned against us. We're told we mustn't flaunt ourselves. We are blamed for encouraging rape by the way we dress. For being too friendly. For being a woman. Not surprisingly, we're confused.

Jane from Basildon said one male friend remarked after she had been indecently assaulted: 'What can you expect, the way you dress?' She comments, 'He was downright awful to me and I retaliated at the time by saying I always wore long skirts anyway, but then that's hardly the point, is it?'

One girl who arrived home in a state of shock and distress after being assaulted, received no sympathy from her father and brother who said she had 'provoked' it by being out alone late at night.

There are other common misconceptions: that women often make false allegations against innocent men; that it couldn't happen without the co-operation of the woman and that she should fight for 'her honour', in which case there would always be evidence of force. Not to resist is 'shameful'. The attitudes linger on and can be seen as the source of the guilt experienced by women who have been raped, and the suspicion of others. These notions pervade society from the classroom to the courtroom.

In cases of rape the tendency to blame victims is extreme: women have been accused of leading men on; 'There's no smoke without fire', said one thirty-year-old man. In a research study, carried out by Christine Howe in Scotland, it was found that a considerable number of people agreed with the statement 'most women who are raped ask for it by the way they dress' and placed a lot of responsibility on the victim. There is a philosophy in life that we get what we deserve, and it would seem people apply this to rape but rarely to other violent crimes. If someone is robbed on the street it is unlikely you'll hear anyone say, 'Well, she's had it coming to her.' The element of blame and the sense of 'defilement' leads to a stigma surrounding rape and its victims:

> Even though I think quite strongly that all women should come forward so that the true face of rape can be revealed, I feel quite frightened about revealing my identity. I was appalled by the reaction of a probation officer in the area (a very senior officer, in fact) who advised me not to disclose to people that I'd been raped, as though I was the criminal. Another person (a woman at the hospital where I work) came up to me a week after the rape and told me that it served me right for picking up a hitchhiker. I hadn't, but that was hardly the point.

Rape is one of the few crimes where the victim is the one who feels guilty, the one who feels ashamed.

Feeding fantasies

The attitudes which see women as provocative yet passive, subordinate yet responsible, are supported by society. Films and video which show violence against women are commonplace and accepted. Not just through private cinema clubs or under-the-counter video sales. These images are seen in films on public release and even on the weekly soap opera. Rape rates highly in the 'entertainment' stakes: too often the 'hero' forcefully overcomes the young woman's resistance . . . the scene fades . . . the next morning she is gazing longingly into his eyes . . . Don't forget, almost every best-seller has its own version of the rape scene!

Many films promote the image of women as subordinate, in a position of being terrorized. *Dressed to Kill*, *When a Stranger Calls*, *Straw Dogs* and countless others have become the focus of controversy. Some argue that this type of film provides an outlet for people who might otherwise become sex offenders, but there have been examples of rapists acting out fantasies they've seen in porn films or magazines. It was said that 'The Fox' rapist started attacking women after seeing a 'blue' movie called *Sex Wish* which showed a violent rape by a man wearing a balaclava and carrying a shotgun. The film was available on video and Conservative M.P. Jill Knight said at the time, 'It is horrendous that a film like this is so easily available. I'm not saying that everyone who sees it will be affected by it. But if just one person goes out and imitates it in the way "The Fox" has, then that is reason enough for action.'

Women are taking action. The campaign group WAVAW (Women Against Violence Against Women) launched attacks on cinemas showing such films, and against video shops renting out porn movies. Films on video, like *Sex Wish*, come under Section Three of the Obscene Publications Act whereby the film can be confiscated (but the shop owners and distributors are not prosecuted), and there is a 'Restricted 18' category used by the film censors which means certain films can only be shown at cinema clubs or segregated cinemas and applications must be made for a special licence. But many believe these films should be banned completely. Research has shown men's attitudes to women are affected by the films they watch, and seeing male dominance and violence on screen makes it more acceptable in real life.

In advertising, too, women are often seen as just another 'commodity' used to sell products: near-naked women were once a regular feature at motor car and boat trade shows, and sexist ads are not restricted to porn magazines but can stare down at you while you're waiting for a train. As such, they appear as accepted images – women whose sole function is to please men – *unless* we campaign against them. You can protest officially about advertisements that use male violence against women by writing to the Advertising Standards Authority (see Resource section).

Strip clubs further the image of women as objects of pleasure for men. Stripping may not degrade the women who do it for a living (who describe the feeling of power and superiority they have over their audience) but it does degrade women as a whole. Pornographic magazines do the same, although to a limited audience. Yet perhaps the most widely seen example of sexist material, with which millions come into contact over the breakfast table, is 'Page Three': a topless female, often featured alongside a report of a violent rape in which the offender is referred to as a beast or fiend, a monster or maniac, or glamourized as 'the six-foot Romeo', while the woman may be described as a 'disco girl', 'a good-time girl', or 'a mother of three' to suggest guilt or innocence. Rape sells newspapers and it is often sensationalized:

one national newspaper ran a four-page pull-out on the exclusive personal story of a woman once married to a rapist.

The concept of rape is often distorted: promoting the myths that the rapist is usually a stranger and likely to be black and that it is an act committed by a maniac at knifepoint, not a boyfriend/girlfriend situation where force takes over: it would be assumed that this would be a 'natural' thing.

As a woman who wrote to a Letters Page put it, 'I don't understand why people are shocked by "the plague of rape". As soon as sex became a subject in schools there were more schoolgirl pregnancies and abortions than you could number. It is only natural that when boys are taught something they want to try it.'

It is difficult to change attitudes which have been instilled for centuries: man the predator, woman the prey. Women have long been seen as the property of men.

Whose body?

Rape has even been seen as a way of controlling and humiliating men (sic). In history, women have been used as a target to get back at men. Soldiers would rape the enemy's women just as they would burn down houses, as a sign of victory and contempt.

The essence of rape was the theft of or damage to another man's property, be it the father or the husband. As a result, rape was originally connected to property, the seizing and devaluing of a possession. In particular, the idea of a virgin daughter was seen as a valuable commodity. If the daughter was raped, her virginity and marriage prospects were gone. The laws of rape were to safeguard men who were afraid that family wealth could be lost through rape and subsequent pregnancy. This helps to explain why rape has always been seen as a more serious crime than indecent assault which, although can cause as much trauma for the woman, does not result in the loss of virginity. Since the Middle Ages the penalty for rape was 'loss of life' but this was only the case where the woman involved was a virgin. Incredibly, this ancient ruling is seen in the attitudes of today where it is still considered to be more of an offence against a woman who is a virgin or sexually inexperienced than it is against a prostitute who is seen as the property of all men. Loss of virginity in some families, where arranged marriages are regarded as important, is still seen as a disaster, and rape as bringing disgrace on the whole family. Sometimes to cover up the disgrace, an arranged marriage may be rushed through or revenge taken. In 1985 a case came to court involving a Sikh father who could not stand the shame when his teenage daughter was raped and her marriage prospects gone. The whole thing brought disgrace on the family and the father thought it was his duty to seek revenge. He arranged the murder of the rapist.

Perhaps the most blatant example of ancient laws having relevance to the law today is that of rape in marriage. One hundred years ago it was legal for a husband to beat his wife and, although laws have changed since then, it is still felt that what goes on within the marital 'four walls' is not the concern of outsiders. Women are, as such, still seen as the husband's property and that he has certain conjugal rights. A woman cannot accuse her husband of rape as he cannot, in theory, take something which already 'belongs' to him. The idea of wives as dependent and submissive is just one of many attitudes which emanate from the law; law which is steeped in opinions and values that used to prevail many years ago and which, it would seem, persist today.

Rape in law

The law relating to rape is contained in the Sexual Offences Act 1956, the Sexual Offences (Amendment) Act 1976 and the Sexual Offences Act 1985 for England and Wales. The 1976 Act states that rape is when a man has unlawful sexual intercourse with a woman without her consent, and at that time knows that she does not consent to the intercourse or is reckless as to whether or not she consents to it. In Scotland it is a common law crime (based on unwritten rules) and there is no statutory definition. Rape is 'the carnal knowledge of a female by a male person obtained by overcoming her will' and it must be proved that the woman's will was overcome by the degree of violence used. In the Republic of Ireland it is contained in the Criminal Law Amendment Act 1935 and the Criminal Law (Rape) Act 1981 and defined as 'unlawful carnal knowledge without a woman's consent.'

To constitute an offence of rape there must be penetration of the vagina by penis (penetration of the outer labia [outer lips] is sufficient). There does not need to be proof of ejaculation. It has to be proven that the woman either physically resisted or, if she did not, that her understanding and knowledge were such that she was not in a position to decide whether to consent or resist. It can also constitute rape if she consents through fear of death, violence or duress, or by fraud such as where a woman consents to sexual intercourse where the man leads her to believe he is performing a medical examination, or that he is her husband. It is also rape if a man has intercourse with a woman who is asleep or unconscious at the time and he is aware of that state; or if a woman is so mentally defective or young (under sixteen) so as to be unable to understand the nature of the act, and therefore not able to resist or consent.

The maximum sentence for rape is life imprisonment and, if convicted, the man is imprisoned in the majority of cases, but generally to a much shorter term than the maximum, from two to seven years.

The rape of young women is often covered as incest: if a woman is raped by her father, brother, grandfather or son the charge brought is incest, not rape, and the maximum sentence is life (if the girl is under thirteen) or seven years (if the girl is over thirteen) compared with the maximum life sentence for all cases of rape.

If there is insufficient evidence to prove penetration (by medical examination) but it can be proven that the man had intended to rape, the charge may be attempted rape (the maximum sentence was seven years in England and Wales until September 1985 when it was made the same maximum sentence as rape: life) or indecent assault, which we shall deal with on page 48.

The maximum sentence of life is also possible when a man has unlawful sexual intercourse with a girl under the age of thirteen and, if it can be proven that intercourse took place, guilt is automatic as the girl is too young to consent. Sometimes this law is used rather than relating to rape, which involves the woman having to prove she did not consent (unless the man pleads guilty). This could therefore lessen the court ordeal for a young girl.

Apart from rape within the family, any man can be convicted of rape unless he is under a certain age (fourteen in England and Wales, fifteen in Ireland, and eight in Scotland) or if he is your husband.

Rape in marriage

Married women are denied a right to which all other women are entitled. According to seventeenth-century legal precedent, 'The husband cannot be guilty of rape committed by himself upon his lawful wife, for by their mutual matrimonial consent and contract the wife has given herself in this kind unto her husband which she cannot retract.' This was amended in 1934, with the provision that he may not use 'physical violence', though if he does he is still not guilty of rape, and in 1974, prohibited when a separation order or a court order or a non-cohabiting clause or order, or an injunction is in effect. The assumption is that having consented once to sex, you have consented forever. A husband cannot be charged with rape of the woman he is married to unless they are legally separated or divorced (a decree nisi granted at least six weeks before the decree absolute effectively terminates a marriage and, therefore with it, consent to marital intercourse) or unless a domestic violence injunction has been granted to the woman against her husband. While rape in marriage is legal, violence is not, and a charge can be brought for grievous bodily harm or a related offence.

The legality of rape in marriage assumes a woman's body is not her own, an assumption which is present in many rape cases. If women have sole rights over their bodies, only one issue remains and that is consent. If rape in marriage was made illegal it would acknowledge that rape can take place between *any* man and woman who are known to each other.

Any woman should have the right to say 'no' in any situation.

It was hoped that the Criminal Law Revision Committee (set up in 1959 to examine and consider revisions to certain aspects of criminal law in England and Wales) would recommend to the government in its report in April 1984 that rape in marriage should be made a crime. The Committee was split over the issue and made no definite recommendation: a sizeable minority urged that a woman should not be denied the protection of the law simply because the man who raped her was her husband, while others on the Committee (made up of seventeen lawyers and judges – just two of them women) pointed out difficulties in proving rape in marriage and said that the criminal law should keep out of the 'marital bed', except where injury arises (in which case other offences can be brought), and that it would be detrimental to marriage as an institution.

Most women believe rape in marriage should be made a crime in all cases where a man has sexual intercourse with his wife without her consent, whether they are separated or not. But it has been left to Parliament to decide. Women Against Rape hope it will take note of the feelings of women: eighty-three per cent think rape in marriage should be a crime, according to the Women's Safety Survey. Just because investigation would not be easy and so it would be difficult to prove without other evidence (most likely physical injury), that should not be a reason for not making it illegal. Most cases of rape are difficult to prove. As Women Against Rape say in *The Rapist Who Pays the Rent* (evidence submitted to the Criminal Law Revision Committee): 'Every person's sexual life is a personal and private matter, but when that sexual life includes rape, it is then a matter for public concern and must not be guarded from public sanction. A man's home may be his castle but this doesn't mean that he should be able to make it a prison for women and children . . . where rape in marriage is concerned, the law not only fails to protect the woman, it actively takes the side of the rapist.'

In Scotland a husband *can* be accused of raping his wife; in the same way it is possible in many other countries around the world, although there are usually limitations. The countries where it may be possible to bring a prosecution of rape in marriage are most of the Communist bloc, Scandinavia and within some Australian and American states.

The legislation in New South Wales was partly prompted by a survey which revealed that thirteen per cent of the women who had been raped had been raped by their husbands. In Russia, Switzerland and Yugoslavia it is an inprisonable offence to coerce a woman into sex by abusing her position of economic dependence or subordination. In Russia this includes the coercion of wives, but in all cases it does depend to what extent and how such rulings are put into practice.

There is still a long way to go, and until rape in marriage is recognized by the law, many believe women's rights in rape and in other areas will not alter.

Indecent assault

Anything other than penetration (and attempted penetration) by the man's penis of the vagina or anus (which is called buggery and carries a maximum life sentence) is called indecent assault. As such it covers a huge 'grey' area without any real clear definition, from having your bottom pinched to serious vaginal or anal penetration with the whole hand or fist, or objects such as bottles or sticks. Because this is treated less seriously than rape, in law, the assumption is it is a lesser offence, but it can be *more* humiliating, and degrading, leading to *more* pain and injury than the assault which is recognized in law as rape. Many believe the definition of rape should be extended to include penetration of the vagina by anything and include anal or oral rape, and so be punishable with the maximum life sentence. But there have been no recommendations to do so, and in the Criminal Law Revision Committee's report it recommended that indecent assault should be seen in law as distinct from rape. The maximum sentence for indecent assault in England and Wales was, until recently, two years' imprisonment where the woman was over thirteen, and five years' imprisonment where under thirteen. Whereas the maximum sentence for indecent assault of a man was set at ten years! This glaring anomaly was cleared up in 1985 and now the same maximum sentence of ten years can be imposed for assaults on both men and women. This is the same as in the Republic of Ireland, while in Scotland it can be sentenced as severely as rape.

A time for change

The law is moving forward, although at a slow pace. But all changes in law must be backed up with a change in attitude for them to have any real impact. Perhaps the solution lies in re-educating – talking to people about the real nature of rape and sexual assault? Schools and colleges are in a prime position to influence and, although there has been resistance in the past, Rape Crisis Centres say their approaches to talk in schools are no longer met with such hostility. Birmingham Rape Crisis Centre: 'While our first priority is to provide a first-class counselling service, our other main aim is to change attitudes in promoting informed views on rape and related issues. If we are going to re-educate we have to start in schools, and hopefully, talking to people about the real nature of rape will improve the prospects of women who have been raped being met with understanding and sympathetic support.'

It is not just the young who need educating, but everyone from the police and doctors to youth club leaders and teachers, to the man and woman in the street. As one woman said, 'The whole area needs to be looked at based on male attitudes towards females and the power structures governing these. It won't go away if women stay in, wear the right clothes and never go anywhere alone. In effect it would disappear. It would be an inapparent crime, as in the majority of cases it already is.'

We need to talk, we need to re-educate, we need to take action.

3

THE CONSTANT FEAR: Taking Action

'When it comes to safety, being a woman is not a good idea.'

Women Against Rape volunteer.

'When I was looking for a flat, I realized I was only considering those on the main road with traffic belting past and bright lights, because I'd have been afraid anywhere else.'

Sandra, 23, from Brighton.

'I find it completely unjust that women cannot go out alone after dark. If it's not men trying to assault you, then it's kerb crawlers. This has happened many times – even in broad daylight.'

Helen, 30, from Bristol.

While men and women may worry about having their purse or wallet snatched in the street, the fear of a sexual attack is almost exclusively female. In fact, women fear rape or other sexual attacks more than almost any other crime, and this is most evident among young women living in large cities.

Yet it is believed that the number of rapes in relation to the number of possible victims is still extremely small and so fears are exaggerated to an extent that the fear itself ends up as more of a problem than the actual danger.

However, exaggerated or not, our worry is very real and many of us modify our actions, even as far as staying at home rather than going out. A report carried out by the Greater London Council's Women's Committee found that nearly eight out of every ten women do not feel safe to go out at night. More than one in three *never* go out alone after dark.

It is likely that these figures are reflected all over Britain, particularly in inner-city areas.

Fear can have the effect of completely taking over – as it did for Jenny. She lives in North London and became a 'prisoner' in her own home, particularly after some of her college friends had been attacked:

> I will never travel alone on buses or trains alone and, before I can make any plans, I have to arrange for a friend to accompany me. Any kind of social life is impossible. I can't go to the pub for a night out, or arrange to meet friends outside the cinema after work, because I won't put myself at risk by walking through the streets or travelling on buses alone. Everything revolves around my fear. You have only to read the newspapers each day to realize that, if you haven't experienced some kind of assault nowadays, then you are incredibly lucky.

Jenny is not alone in the way she feels. Other women express the same fears:

> I won't go out at night and I really hate being at home on my own when the rest of the family is out. I'm more afraid now, as my mum and dad are getting divorced and there's no man about the house for 'protection'. I don't even go out in the daytime unless it's somewhere built-up and I know the area well. I'm also learning to drive at the moment but, when I pass, I won't go anywhere on my own as I'd be afraid if the car broke down somewhere isolated. Some of my friends think I'm crazy, but I'm genuinely terrified. *Teresa, 18, from Surrey.*

> Over the years, my awareness of the possibility of rape has dawned on me so much that I'm a lot more fearful of going out at night on my own. Sometimes, I won't even go out in the day if I know it's to an isolated place. It seems crazy that it's only dawned on me now and not in my teens or early twenties. I haven't been raped, but now I live in fear, and it drains me to even think about it. The realization that it can happen almost anywhere is crucifying. In the past, I've hitched alone, lived alone in quiet places, and gone to isolated places alone. Now I do none of these things. I feel my sense of freedom to be crushed, while men do not experience this fear. Their allowance of freedom sickens me.
> *May, from Edinburgh.*

Clearly, it is important not to create a climate of fear, not to make women so afraid that it restricts our lives, but to use that fear to our advantage. By being more aware of risks, women should become more positive, confident and less vulnerable.

Chief Superintendent Sheila Ward, who organizes self-defence courses run by the Metropolitan Police, says: 'We must not make women so frightened by all this that they spend their days in terror. If we do, we're restricting a woman's freedom to go, do and wear what she wants. It's a case of striking the right balance between showing the dangers and yet still living our lives as we choose.'

It's not surprising many women resent limitations on their lifestyle – however, it does make sense to look at what you can do to restore control by taking steps to a 'safer' existence. Often it's just thinking a bit more carefully about what you're doing. For example, don't walk the dog at midnight on a lonely recreation ground . . . Always try to arrange how you'll get home after a night out instead of leaving it till the last minute . . . Perhaps you should alter your way home after work occasionally, by catching a different train or walking another route.

Just as you make your house secure with locks and bolts, you can take steps to help yourself. But, in the same way that a house is never a hundred per cent safe, there is no ten point guaranteed formula to make you safe from rape. Even if you did restrict your lifestyle to the extreme where you might say you'll stay indoors twenty-four hours a day and only invite friends and family to your home – how safe do you think you'd be? Many rapes occur *in* the home and rapists are often known to the victims: a friend or relation.

It doesn't mean we have to be permanently suspicious. Just use your intuition to guide you. If you feel uncomfortable in a certain situation, get out quickly. Often, we don't know who to trust – everyone or no one?

Do we think twice about where we go and who with? The answers may be different for individual women.

The suggestions in this chapter are for every woman who wants to take action. Here, first, is some commonsense advice for women who have felt fear in walking alone:

- Avoid dimly lit streets, alleyways, dark, deserted areas and short cuts. Walk the long way round rather than cross a common. When walking along a street, use the side of the pavement nearest the road – or, if there is no traffic, walk in the middle of the road.

- Walk on the right hand side of the road against the direction of traffic. If you sense a car is following you, turn and run in the opposite direction; it'll make it difficult for the driver to follow. Don't run in the same direction as the car – it only has to speed up.
- Walk confidently, look as though you know where you're going, and be aware of everything around you. American research showed that people are more at risk from attack if they *appear* fearful, unsure or 'dreamy'. Confidence can be one of the best methods of defence and can be conveyed in your walk. That alone can deter an attacker.
- Police implore women not to hitchhike. If you really must, only accept lifts from other women. Do not accept a lift because the driver seems 'nice'.
- If you sense you're being followed, go into the nearest pub, petrol station or shop and ask for help or phone a friend who lives nearby; if you're really worried, phone the police. If everything is closed, bang on a house door where you see a light on (but don't expect people always to help). If there is nowhere to run to, turn and face the man; you'll take away one of his major weapons – surprise.
- Either wear shoes in which you can run or be prepared to kick them off and run. Be aware that a scarf around your neck could be used against you.
- Better to look foolish than risk being raped. Don't be embarrassed – do anything you can to get help or attract attention. Trust your instinct and err on the side of caution.

Note: Men, too, should be aware that if walking behind a woman, she may assume she is being followed. They should cross over or take a different route.

The reason why so many women have to resort to walking or

hitching is often because of lack of money and poor public transport. Women sometimes have to travel at odd times – perhaps working shifts – and cannot always be choosy about the location and/or hours of jobs they manage to get. Few have their own cars and most cannot afford minicabs so have to rely on poor or irregular transport. In rural areas it's often worse: buses stop running early in the evening and, in some places, there are no buses at all so, unless you drive, you either walk or hitch.

One young girl tells how she continued to hitch lifts even after police warnings and the rape of a seventeen-year-old girl in her village after she had accepted a lift from a stranger on the way home from a party. Her reason: 'It's very remote and lonely around here. There are hardly any buses and nothing at all late at night. What alternative is there? Hitching is the only way . . .'

Ask any woman and most will tell you they have hitchhiked on at least one occasion. The alternative may have been walking home or, if public transport was running, a long wait at a bus stop, dark walks to and from the tube station, and sitting on empty platforms and in carriages alone.

Other women make a different choice: they stay at home.

No-woman's land

Before a woman can go out, she has to think how she is going to get there and arrange how to get back home again. Many attacks take place in the hours from 6 pm to 1 am, when women are making their way home from working late, or are forced to walk home as they've missed the last bus.

From badly lit streets in large cities to desolate country lanes, all are danger zones for the woman alone.

Traditionally, women have little control over the environment: London, and most major cities and towns, are planned by men for men. The safety of women is secondary or of little significance.

Town planners have created a situation of no-woman's land: shopping precincts at night, deserted and badly-lit open spaces, alleyways, no-through roads, narrow pathways and subways. Well-lit bridges and walkways are safer than subways but, where they exist, they should have wide, open approaches, be well lit and, when possible, fitted with closed-circuit television. Better lighting, with vandal-proof fittings – particularly in side streets – is thought to be one of the most essential factors for making women safer. Badly-lit places provide safe refuge for prowlers/attackers, who might think twice if they knew they were visible.

> A woman's freedom is being taken away. Men can just get up and go out when they feel like it. If my husband suddenly decides he is going down the road to the pub or to see a friend, he just gets up, puts on his coat and goes. *I* have to think about whether I should go and how I'll get home. If I'm walking along a road and someone's behind me, I'm conscious the whole time that they're there. I constantly keep one eye over my shoulder – I have to. When I'm sitting on a bus or train, particularly at night, I'm looking around all the time to see what's happening. I make a mental note of where the emergency cord is, too. I try to carry a book or paper and, once I think I know where everyone's sitting, I keep my head down low. But I'm still aware of any slight movement.
>
> *Mary, 38, from London.*

The first ever survey concerned specifically with the transport needs and problems of women was carried out by the Women's Committee of the Greater London Council, and found that, like Mary, many women felt unsafe on public transport, particularly at night when seventy per cent said they felt unsafe waiting for buses at badly lit stops in isolated places and choose to walk rather than 'wait for the bus that never comes'.

There is much that can be done: including more reliable timetables and more buses (particularly in the evenings). Women feel particularly at risk on trains and station platforms because of the shortage of staff, who are being replaced by fully automated ticket machines.

Stations become an attacker's paradise. For a start, more platform staff are needed, particularly at night: any woman who has waited on a deserted station platform for a train will express the fear of isolation.

One woman was subjected to sexual assault on Charing Cross tube station and wrote in a national newspaper: 'I was aware of a group of rowdy men who had obviously been having a good night out on the town, so I buried my head even deeper in my book and ignored them. The next thing I knew, I was knocked flat on the bench by a man landing heavily on top of me. I was subjected to a humiliating and degrading sexual assault, culminating in having a vibrator forced into my mouth. The clothing I was wearing – which the men had great difficulty in undoing – probably saved me from greater physical abuse. Only when I burst into tears did one of them come to his senses and drag me out from under his associates. The reason I didn't go to the police station when I reached my destination will probably be understood by all women who have been in this situation: I had not been raped, I had not been beaten up, I had not been robbed, I had been used – a woman alone at night – as a target for their manly fun and games.'

Less staff reduces a woman's security. As it is, travelling by trains, underground and buses puts women into situations without a means of exit immediately available and where they are isolated from other people: a platform, a pedestrian subway, emergency stairs, a train compartment.

Panic buttons should be installed within easy reach on trains (and also on the upper decks of buses) which do not stop the train in the tunnel but alert platform staff at the next station and allow you to talk to the driver. Closed-circuit televisions could also be installed on platforms and emergency stairs, with direct connection to staff.

Some tube stations already have closed-circuit television, and little-used subways are closed. The possibility of fewer carriages on off-peak hour trains is being investigated.

One of the biggest dangers is the closed-off compartments which are still used in certain areas of the country, particularly on the Southern Region. Indeed, these compartments aided that attacker known as the Railway Rapist, caught in 1985, to carry out a series of attacks, one on the Dartford to Charing Cross line between stations.

British Rail intend to phase these out completely in favour of the walk-through carriages.

A suggestion made by the campaigning group Safe Women's Transport is for women-only carriages, or one 'secure' carriage per train at night – in which staff are available to give extra protection.

In the Women and Transport Survey, sixty-one per cent of

women thought women-only carriages would improve safety. Ironically, single-sex compartments were introduced by BR over eighty years ago. In that instance, the origin of the Ladies Only carriages, as they were known, stemmed from Victorian decency rather than concern over safety. The last of these were withdrawn in the mid 1960s, and there are no plans to bring them back, despite the strong feelings of women.

The opposition takes the approach that women-only carriages would cause disruption in the rush hour and would indicate to anyone out to cause trouble that here are women travelling and susceptible to attack.

It would be important too for women not to feel they *had* to use them and that if they sat in another carriage then it was assumed they were asking to be raped. That would be like saying: 'We have battered wives' refuges, so if a woman doesn't choose to live in one, then she deserves to be battered!'

With no plans to bring in these carriages, the only advice given to women is to try and sit in an open carriage with other women or near the guard. The problem with sitting near the guard is that you can then end up isolated on the platform when you leave the train, as the guard's van is usually situated in the last carriage.

Much more needs to be done, particularly by local and public transport authorities. As it is, women have to rely on their own sense of survival, and on community projects and volunteer schemes being set up in response to women's fears.

In some major cities, including London, and in particular on university campuses, efforts have been made to offer women a completely safe alternative with door-to-door transport. Colleges in Leeds, Oxford and in many other cities arrange minibuses for students to use after late-night lectures.

At Oxford Polytechnic the Student Union organized a minibus for a whole term and set up rotas with people meeting in the main hall to go home together. The problem was getting women to use it: most seemed to think they didn't need it, as 'it wasn't going to happen to them'.

The Stockwell Lift Service was started in 1982 to provide safe transport for women in South Clapham and Brixton. At first, it was run from a community flat by volunteers at weekends, and has since received a grant to enable it to operate more effectively. It works by being more flexible than a bus, because it picks up women from their homes and takes them back. It also features certain regular trips, such as advanced bookings from groups to take them to evening classes or to pick them up from a disco.

In areas where something like that may not be possible, an alternative is to get together with some friends and set up a small-scale transport scheme. For example, in a rural area a group of women could share the costs of a car and arrange to travel together.

You should put pressure on your local authority and write to your MP, making it clear that it is essential that something be done about the public transport in your area.

You could also suggest that the company you work for takes a more active role in the safety of its staff, particularly where shift work and irregular hours are involved.

Local initiative is good but authorities should do more. We should not have to rely on community projects and volunteers.

Safety drive

Few women have their own car or free access to a car, and most women do not have driving licences. But even if you have a car or can afford a taxi, there is still the time between leaving a vehicle and entering the building when you are vulnerable to attack. Irene thought she was safe:

> I always made sure I locked the garage for safety, but I'd been in such a rush that morning I must have forgotten. When I drove home that night I went to unlock it and was concerned to find it already open. I drove in, got out of the car, and someone grabbed me round the neck. I swung round and saw a man wearing a brown balaclava and holding an iron bar. He forced me back into the car, raped me and ran. The whole thing must have been over in about ten minutes. He didn't say a word and I was too scared to resist. I'd bought the car as I worked shifts and hated travelling on trains late at night. Now I'm even frightened to go out in the car unless I'm with someone else.

If you drive, here are some points to remember . . .

- If you sense someone is following you in another car, *don't* drive home. Drive, instead, to the local police station or to a busy area and sound your horn until someone comes to help.
- If you're sitting in your car, waiting, check all the doors are locked. The same applies if driving through town where you may have to stop at traffic lights, etc. Always check your locks and keep them in good working order. (One woman, whose car had faulty locks, stopped to help a 'stranded' motorist and he pushed his way into her car.) Always keep your garage locked.
- Do not stop to help a stranded motorist. Instead, drive to the next telephone and call for assistance or phone when you get home to report there is a broken-down car.
- Park in busy, well-lit areas and always lock your car. If you will not be returning to your car till some time later, consider carefully where you park. It may be a busy area during the day because of shops, etc, but deserted at night. Even if it's daylight when you park, try to park under a street lamp near houses rather than shops in case you return when it's darker.
- When returning to your car, have the keys ready so you don't waste time fumbling for them. Before you get in, check the car is empty. Then, once inside, lock the doors.
- As far as possible, travel on main or well-used roads.

Home sweet home

More of us are living alone than ever before. Between 1961 and 1980, one-person households doubled and they are still on the increase. Some say that by 1990 one-third of British people will be living alone, and it is that which often makes women feel most at risk.

Women tend to spend more time at home than men, either because they do not work outside the home, or have a part-time job, and many express feeling vulnerable as much during the *daytime indoors*, as being *outdoors at night*.

There are some steps you can take to feel safer in your home against the intruder who may be a rapist . . .

- Don't 'advertise' the fact that you live alone by using your Christian name on the doorbell or in the phone book. Use your initial. If someone phones as a wrong number, don't tell them yours but ask what number they wanted. Never mention, inadvertently, that you live alone: 'There's no one here called Fred. I should know, I'm the only one in this house!'
- Have a safety chain and spy-hole fitted, and ensure all windows and doors are secure.
- If your handbag containing your keys is stolen, change the locks, even if your address is not in your bag – the thief could follow you home. If moving into a new home, you should also change the locks, as you never know who may have been given a key by the previous owners.
- Have your keys ready to open the door quickly and easily when returning home.
- Don't let people into the house just because they're wearing a uniform and say they've come to read the meter. Keep the chain on the door while you ask them for some form of identification. If in any doubt, phone the company to check if they have sent anyone on an official visit. If you're unsure, tell them to come another time.
- Draw curtains and blinds after dark or, if you're going to be out late, fit a light which is switched on by a timer.
- Never leave knives or scissors lying about at home, where an intruder could easily grab them to use as a weapon against you.
- If you find doors or windows tampered with as you approach your home, or see someone suspicious standing near your entrance, don't go inside. Phone the police from a call box or go to your neighbours to ask for help.
- If you're at home and think you have an intruder, or you hear strange noises outside your home, leave as quickly as possible. If you need to, do not hesitate to break a window to attract attention.

This guide may help against the rapist who is the intruder or the stranger, but many rapes which happen in the home are not the result of forced entry. It can be a man you've invited in, or share a flat with, your husband, a relation. Very often, the only option then is not to secure yourself *in* the home but to get *out*. Easier said than done, though. The reason most women stay in situations of sexual violence is because they have nowhere else to go.

The Housing (Homeless Persons) Act 1977 gives women the right to be rehoused if they leave home due to domestic violence but, even then, local authorities frequently fail to do so. The most common excuse is that the woman cannot show visible bruising or produce evidence of assault, which would often be the case with rape in marriage.

In a report carried out in all the refuges in England and Wales by the Women's Aid Federation, titled *Leaving Violent Men*, the most common feeling expressed by women who had experienced sexual abuse or violence was the lack of options open to them.

Where a woman is in danger of rape, so, too, are her children. If she doesn't have the money to leave, then she doesn't have the money to take her children away if they are the ones in danger.

Instead of the situation getting better, it is getting worse: local councils are having their funding cut back and, along with the cuts in council house building and the sale of existing properties, there are less and less alternatives on offer.

Love thy neighbour

The effect of cutbacks on spending has an effect on halting many things which need to be done to help women feel safer going about their business and in their homes. Fear for personal safety is particularly great among women living in council housing, where the need for improved security, such as stronger front doors, better locks and hinges, entryphones and caretakers, is often pushed to the end of the list when it comes to allocating funds.

In certain areas, streets and estates have set up Neighbourhood Watch Schemes (details on setting up these from your local police station) in which the local people get together to 'fight' crime, including rape. The idea is that everyone 'watches' each other's home and reports anything suspicious. Some set up a kind of agreed alarm system, such as a whistle or certain call which means you need help – and fast!

It's a good idea to get neighbours to talk about helping each other, as it is, sadly, true that often people don't want to get involved and ignore cries for help. Some claim they thought it was a domestic squabble and didn't want to get involved.

One man who was witness to a rape attack said in court: 'I heard a woman shouting "Rape" three times, and heard her saying, "No, No." Then I saw a couple struggling and the man pulled the woman over a fence and behind a wall. I thought it was a domestic argument and didn't do anything about it.'

The screams of another woman continued for ten hours. Neighbours heard but did nothing. The rapist broke into her flat, tied her up, and blindfolded her and then raped her at knifepoint. Her ordeal lasted 10 hours – she was raped three times – and her screams and sobs woke her neighbour who said he turned up the radio to cover all the noise. When it continued he shouted to ask if the girl was all right but, although she did not reply, he did nothing. The High Court judge said at the case: 'If people took a little more notice of what went on around them there would be less crime. The English habit of turning a deaf ear to what happens can lead to terrifying results.'

Screaming doesn't necessarily mean anyone will come to your aid – even if they hear you. People say they thought it was children 'messing about'. You might find passers-by more likely to help if you shout 'Fire!' than if you shout 'Rape!'

If you ever hear anyone calling for help, or see people acting suspiciously, don't ignore it. Be prepared to go to the aid of others.

Better to be told to 'clear off' than read the next day in the newspapers that a woman has been raped. Report *anything* you think suspicious.

Police in Oxford talk to students at the Polytechnic and encourage them to report everything and anything: 'If you see someone sitting in a car, looking suspicious, just call. Even if it turns out to be the local vicar, you'll have done the right thing,' said a female officer.

In Oxford they have a special unit dealing with everything from flashers to rape. The way to react to flashers is to walk by, ignore them and, most importantly, to report them. Flashers often turn out to be someone wanted by the police for other sex offences, as do kerb-crawlers.

Chief Superintendent Sheila Ward of the Metropolitan Police is continually urging people to take notice of what's going on around them: 'As a society, we have got to show we disapprove. It is intolerable to think people will ignore violent attacks to the extent that they can happen in broad daylight with crowds nearby – and we let them get away with it.'

If you see someone being pestered, don't walk on. Often, just walking towards them causes the assailant to run off, says Sheila Ward. 'I was on a tube platform one night. It was pretty deserted and there was a woman sitting alone on one of the benches. A young man came along, sat next to her and it was obvious he was starting to move too close to her. I got up and walked down to where they were, and another young couple did the same. It was enough to make it clear we disapproved. He leapt up and ran off.'

It often takes a rape attack or a series of assaults to shock people into action. At the time of the 'Yorkshire Ripper', people got together to share cars and put each other up overnight. When the 'Fox' rapist struck in the tiny villages of Bedfordshire, men and women got together to arrange 'vigilante' patrols and families moved into each other's homes for security.

Jayne lives in a small close-knit community in Nottinghamshire, and says how easy it is to become apathetic:

> You get this false sense of security, living in a village where everyone is known to you. You think things like murder and rape just don't happen.
>
> I was walking to a friend's house one evening in October, when I was aware of a car following me – or so it seemed. I was not really suspicious at the time and just thought the driver had lost his way round the village. But, later, when I left my friend's house, I saw the car again, cruising up and down the road. I made a mental note of the car's registration and, fortunately, managed to lose him at the bottom of my friend's street.
>
> The next morning, I was devastated to hear on the local news that a friend I'd known since the age of seven had been killed: her body had been found in a field adjoining a country lane leading

out of the village. She had been sexually assaulted and strangled.

I phoned the police, told them what had happened to me and the registration number Apparently, several young girls had been followed by the same driver on the previous night, but not one of us had informed the police until hearing about the murder. The police were in no doubt that the man who followed me was the murderer; the same car (which had been stolen) had also been spotted near the place where my friend's body was found.

I wish to God I'd reported that man before it was too late. The man you suspect may be perfectly respectable and he may have lost his way, but the chance is always there . . .

Take up arms

Women cannot rely on other people for protection or aid, so many carry objects with them which could be used for their defence: a can of hairspray, keys poked through the knuckles, a telescopic umbrella, a lit cigarette, a rolled magazine – and keep in mind how they could use them. A handbag can be full of potential weapons, as can a shopping bag: perfume sprayed in the eyes of an attacker can temporarily blind him; a comb to scrape across the face; a nail file or stiletto heel; a tin of food or a bottle to swing. The handbag itself, if heavy enough, can be an effective weapon, as is the old-fashioned hat pin.

Mini shriek alarms can be carried, especially designed to give out an ear-piercing siren when activated. They are all well and good but women tend to carry them in their bags and it takes several minutes to get them out. Even then, they are only effective if people are around to hear and are prepared to take any notice or react to your call for help.

On the continent there are specially designed anti-rape weapons which are illegal here. The Women's Safety Survey showed that nine out of ten London women want the legal right to carry weapons for self defence. Many said they were already breaking the law by carrying such weapons: a pot of pepper, knives, a screwdriver, ammonia, metal tubing, even coins in a sock.

However, you can be charged with carrying an offensive weapon if you deliberately have an object in your possession for the purpose of defence. The problem with all weapons is that it is alien to most women to use them, and there is also the danger that they may be put to use against you, particularly if you don't know how to use them properly. One woman had a spray repellent but the wind blew it in *her* face. Another used a hairspray but had no time to check which way it was directed and sprayed it in her own face instead.

Carol was touring South America with a friend when she was raped:

> We always had big Bowie knives with us but they were only to make sandwiches and things like that! We were sleeping in our tent on a deserted camp site when we were attacked. We had our knives by us – which is just about the worst thing you can do in that situation, especially if you don't know how to use them. There were four of them and one of them accidentally, we think, slashed my friend's leg from the thigh to the knee with her own knife. We didn't realize how badly at the time but, in fact, it was cut to the bone. She had to stay in hospital for a week. It is all very well to say it afterwards but we should have kept our knives packed away – that was the biggest mistake we made.

Our body has its own built-in weapons, too: teeth, fists, nails. But most women find it difficult to put these to use either. It involves a complete change of attitude: becoming *angry* at the way your life is restricted; starting to believe you are *worth* defending; that you have a *right* to do those things you want to do; gaining *self-respect* and *confidence* in your own worth; developing your sense of *survival*.

Kaleghl Quinn, an American self-defence teacher and author of *Stand Your Ground* (Orbis) based on a Channel 4 television series, says we have to learn to defend ourselves: 'Building feelings of self-respect and self-esteem are fundamental to learning not to be a victim. If you don't feel you're worthwhile, valuable, then you won't feel you're worth defending.'

Women, by tradition, are the passive type, not brought up to fight or defend themselves, but the demand for self-defence classes in the last five years has shown that women want to have control, are learning to value themselves, and are prepared to take action.

The Metropolitan Police have witnessed a huge demand for the self-defence courses they have been running since September 1983. Chief Superintendent Sheila Ward says: 'Rather naively, perhaps, we trained fifty people, male and female, to go round in teams of two to give the classes. Demand was so great, we now have 150.'

Opponents argue that we should not counter violence with more violence, but the object of self-defence is evasive action, not offensive. It is all about how to avoid trouble and to get away safely. Some women expressed concern that fighting the attacker would escalate the violence, so have not tried self-defence. Avoiding a dangerous situation is number one priority; self-defence skills are used only when necessary. But even screaming and running away or talking your way out of a situation are self-defence mechanisms: the initial object of self defence is to take some action to give you the chance to escape. Adds Sheila Ward, 'In a violent situation only you can judge the best way out. We're not saying to women you should resist, or not resist. We're saying if it happens and you choose to fight back, you'll know how to if you've done self-defence. But it has to be an individual decision made by each woman when confronted – only you know what to do for the best.'

Self-defence classes differ from those which are solely martial arts and can take years to master. Some still call themselves self-defence, but offer no more than a quick course in judo or karate, and leave women with the false impression that, just because they've learnt a few throws, they're able to defend themselves. Women's self defence is not a martial art and, as such, the requirements are very different. Women wanting to defend themselves on 'street level', don't necessarily aspire to become a black belt in karate, but they do want to 'learn' how to scream – practice makes perfect. Screaming can be one of the most valuable weapons a woman has, but the very fact there are people around does not mean they will come to your aid, and it could make an attacker grab you around the neck and mouth to stifle the scream.

Remember self-defence is not just a set of moves to strike out. The courses are as much to do with self-confidence and assertion as physical strength. It is learning how to use your initiative, creating a greater awareness to assess a situation and see how best you might get away. Be aware and be prepared.

The question most women ask is: 'How should I react if attacked?' There is no one answer. Sometimes, taking the powerful, angry role might frighten the attacker away, shocked that you are prepared to fight back. Or it may cause more damage. An American study found that there is probably a higher chance of getting away if you fight back, but also greater risk of being seriously injured. Some rapists want the woman to struggle so that they can overpower her; therefore, being passive may work or it may, as some women have said, only make the rapist more violent and sadistic in order to incite some kind of reaction from his victim.

You may feel you can talk your way out of a situation. For some women this has worked, by staying calm and talking to the attacker, trying to make him see them as a 'person', asking about his family, etc; or by pretending to be keen for sex but suggesting it happen elsewhere or on another night.

Julie from Manchester:

> There was no one around, so I knew there was no point in screaming for help. I tried to act cool, as though I wasn't frightened at all. He asked me about my boyfriend and I said I hadn't got one but I thought he was nice. I told him I had my period but I'd really like to see him the next night. He actually believed me; I don't think I thought it would work. We arranged to meet in the Wimpy Bar at eight o'clock the next night. I alerted the police, but he never turned up.

This approach might work where the man is young and finds difficulty in forming relationships, but try it with a cold-blooded attacker aroused by violence and you could be playing with fire.

Caroline, from Glasgow, says:

> He told me to get into the back of the car and undress. I said why didn't we go back to my flat instead, as it would be much more comfortable. I knew if I could get him back there, I could alert my friend next door. He smashed my face and told me not to try to be clever with him, that he knew my game.

One woman tried to tell her attacker she had VD. It didn't work.

Another woman at a self-defence class in Oxford told how she escaped being raped after accepting a lift:

> I was trying to get home to my parents in Southampton at the end of term. I'd done it so many times before that, even when I read about girls getting attacked, I never thought it could happen to me. He seemed really nice, had a brand new car, was telling me about his family and his work. After we'd been chatting for about thirty minutes, he started talking about his collection of magazines. It didn't take long to realize he was talking about porn magazines and he opened the compartment and took a couple out. I said I wasn't interested but, very calmly and coldly, he demanded I read them. I don't even remember seeing anything on the pages. All along, I was thinking, 'How do I get out of this one?' He was making lewd suggestions, but I don't remember half of what he said. I even thought about jumping but, at sixty miles an hour on a motorway, it takes more courage than I've got.
>
> Instead, I pretended I was feeling sick. I said reading in cars always made me feel ill since I was a child. At first, he didn't believe me, but I think when he suddenly thought his brand new car was going to be messed up, he agreed to pull into a transport cafe. I went into the toilet, locked myself in and just sat in there for ages – I don't know how long – shaking. I didn't know what to do. I thought if I went out there he'd be waiting for me.
>
> A woman came in and I explained to her what had happened. She was great and took me outside to her husband who phoned the police. But he'd gone, there was no sight of him.

It is difficult to keep a clear head and stay calm in a situation where you feel threatened. Often, just the surprise of sudden contact with another person can send you into a state of shock, so you are unable to respond quickly, unable to cry out for help.

The shock of being struck, or falling over, gives your attacker the advantage. Self-defence classes can teach you how to fall, to land on the fleshy parts of your body, and how, once you're down, to get back up immediately.

It's difficult in a class to relate it to a life and death type situation; falling on a mat can be very different from falling on concrete, just as it's also difficult to create the feeling of fear when you're in a nice, warm, cosy gym surrounded by friends and wearing easy-fitting clothes. Fear will be the natural reaction, so try to create that in your mind: feelings of danger and risk.

A self-defence teacher says: 'We try to get them to feel anger – "What right has this man to do this to me?" – then it's a case of training them to use this anger to their advantage. Anger can be a very constructive passion. You'd know that, if you've seen anyone in cold anger.'

The way to channel fear and release anger and aggression can be learnt with practice and give you strength and confidence. Yet, as well as the psychological barriers, there are those who think self-defence is pointless for them because they're small and weak. But self-defence skills can compensate for lack of muscle power; we are not as helpless as some might have us believe.

You don't have to be at a certain level of fitness or age to take self-defence classes; a frail eighty-year-old should be just as familiar with the techniques as a woman of twenty.

The Metropolitan Police run courses for the blind, elderly and handicapped and their target age group for the general course is middle-aged women, who don't have co-ordination, fitness or much time to spare, and are perhaps self-conscious about going to classes which encourage physical activity. Even so, it's to your advantage to be in good physical condition: regular swimming and jogging increase your agility and stamina, and sports like squash and tennis are good for timing and speeding up your reflexes.

Self-defence is not just about building up muscles, but showing how to employ our natural strengths and use our own in-built weapons: teeth, elbows, feet, nails, fists. It also points out the vulnerable areas of your attacker; muscle power is irrelevant if you know the spots to go for because they are susceptible to the minimum of pressure: fingers poked in the eyes, a kick in the groin, a blow to the nose. Less obvious ones include striking the kidneys, a backward elbow thrust into the bladder area or stabbing with fingers the hollow of the throat.

Even all this knowledge and practice cannot make you 100 per cent safe, but it does mean you'll have more confidence, if it should happen, to strike out.

Whatever you do, it's important any retaliation be carried out with conviction – a half-hearted blow could antagonize an attacker even more.

When you decide on an action, do it swiftly and with force – deliver hard and fast. If you knee him in the groin he should instinctively go to protect himself. Don't wait around to see if he does, but use the few seconds to escape – just run and don't look back. Some women said they waited around to see if it had worked.

Some actions call for quite a bit of nerve: if his head is close to yours, you could try holding the sides of his head with your fingers and use your thumbs to press his eyes in towards the back of his skull. It doesn't take much pressure to cause shock to the brain and a temporary blackout, but will take some nerve on your part to do it. It's quite a different matter to read about it than to put it into practice. There are lots of helpful books, but you really need to go to a class where you can try out techniques.

It's often a good idea to go along with a few friends; not only does it keep up the incentive for going, it creates a shared determination and brings women together. It also means you've got someone to travel to and from the venue with, particularly as they're often evening classes and involve getting home in the dark.

Some schools and colleges run self-defence courses for their pupils, but usually after normal classes, again involving the hazard of getting home on dark evenings in the winter months.

Many women believe it should be taught in all schools, to every female over the age of eleven, as part of the school curriculum, and that companies should be encouraged to organize a self-defence programme for employees: Marks & Spencer were among the first to do this as long ago as November 1980, when they also issued their staff with mini-buzzer alarms.

Police in various forces, such as Thames Valley, are going into colleges to talk to students, to try and encourage a greater awareness, give advice on self-protection and ask that anything suspicious be reported.

Teach-in

For years the Rape Crisis Centres have tried to give talks to children in schools, to make them more aware of the risks of sexual abuse, but, in the past, there has been much opposition. Now, in some areas, the message seems to be getting through:

better to warn them about the risks than wait for the time it's forced upon them.

Often, the argument used by headmasters, teachers and parents was that it was a problem that didn't exist. Only now is the truth of the matter coming out, largely through the work of Michele Elliott, who runs the Child Assault Prevention Programme.

When she first introduced the programme in Britain in 1982 (it first started in America in 1978 in Ohio), it was dismissed: 'They said it was an American problem and, as such, we didn't really need to concern ourselves with it!' says Michele.

Now she is in such demand that she is booked months in advance to go to schools and give talks to children, teachers, social workers and some parents. It is a far greater problem than even she had imagined.

After the workshops and talks to children aged from five to sixteen about sexual abuse, she then invites those who want to talk about it with her privately to stay. One in five children usually has some experience they want to tell her about.

It is estimated that around one in ten children will be sexually abused before the age of sixteen, and over seventy-five per cent of these assaults are carried out by adults known to the child. Yet the police film *Don't Go With a Stranger* doesn't even mention the problem of sexual abuse and, as Michele says: 'To tell children they should watch out only for strangers is like telling them to beware of only red cars when they cross the road.' It's important not to terrify children, but neither can we pretend it doesn't happen.

The methods are simple and effective. Offenders often begin by testing a child's willingness to keep a secret, explains Michele, and take advantage of their vulnerability because they've been brought up to be polite and obedient to adults.

> Instead of teaching your children to listen to and obey all adults unquestioningly, tell them they have your permission and support to say 'no' to protect themselves. Discuss the idea of good and bad secrets. Teach them the difference between a good secret like a birthday party, and a bad secret like someone stealing from a shop. I say to them, 'Your mum and dad don't ask you to keep it a secret when they tuck you up in bed and kiss you goodnight, do they?' So

> they should always tell if they are asked to keep a kiss or cuddle secret, or when the secret makes them feel uncomfortable and confused, or when someone touches their body in a way they don't like.

Michele encourages parents and teachers to become more aware and to watch out for signs which may indicate something is wrong, such as a child suddenly becoming withdrawn or reluctant to visit someone. (We look at these signs more closely in the next chapter.) Even then people are often in the dark as to what they should do for the best:

> Teachers and parents are often uncertain about how they should cope with the problem. The most important thing to start with is to show you believe and support a child who has just confided in you. It takes a lot to get a child to talk about something so intimate, and usually something they don't understand, apart from knowing it makes them very unhappy. Very few children lie about what is happening to the extent of making it all up, but they may say it is their uncle who is abusing them when, in fact, it turns out to be the father.

If you sense something is wrong try to encourage the child to talk, if not to you then to a friend or relative (where possible). 'Often there is no-one they feel they can confide in,' says Michele. 'One little boy came up to me at the end of my workshops and I knew he was troubled but I couldn't get him to tell me exactly what was going on. I said to him that if he couldn't tell me, did he have a friend, or someone at home he thought he could talk to about it. He said he would go home and tell his dog.'

Children can feel very isolated; it must seem they are the only one it is happening to, and often the offender makes the child feel they are to blame for what is happening, or has them in such a 'hold' that they are unable to go to anyone for help. 'It is important they do not feel any guilt,' says Michele. 'I said to one man, who commented that young girls of eleven and twelve can sometimes be provocative, that if his daughter dances naked on the coffee table in front of him, *he* is the one responsible if he abuses her, and he alone.'

Making children more aware of the risks should not be seen as trying to make them responsible for what happens. Heightening awareness should be encouraged, but it should not be seen as transferring responsibility to women and girls for the actions of men. Often suggestions like taking self-defence, fitting a chain to your front door or not accepting lifts from strangers are seen by some people as 'rules' and when women break those rules what can they expect if they get raped? Women cannot take responsibility for rape, and if you choose to ignore this chapter, it doesn't mean you lay yourself open to abuse by men.

It's your decision

Only you can decide how far you follow advice and take precautions. Some women take the view: 'We all lock our front doors at night, secure the car when we leave it parked somewhere, and I don't see how it's any different to be sensible when it comes to protecting your own self.' While others argue: 'Women should not have to think about how they walk home at night, what they wear, where they live. We must not feel that we are the ones who have to take precautions so that we can be safe. Even self-defence is a way of making women responsible for whether or not they are raped.'

But self-defence does mean we can feel more confident to stand up for ourselves, and if men know we're not such easy targets and are likely to give as good as we get, some say we might see a decrease in this type of crime.

Even so, it's important to stress that no woman who takes all the precautions and self-defence classes is automatically safe. No-one can say how or when it may happen, or how you will react. Says Chief Superintendent Sheila Ward: 'Whichever way you respond we would not say it's wrong. As at the end of the day you're the one who has got to cope with the consequences of your action.'

Many women have problems over the way they have reacted, and they are not helped by the attitudes of those around them. Many feel they should have done more, and that feeling stays with them for a long time.

Whatever your feelings after reading this chapter, make use of them. If you feel more alert and more powerful, awareness is a useful ally against fear. If you feel anger, it is a powerful emotion – use it to make your feelings known.

4

THE AFTERMATH:
Reactions and Actions

'You feel so isolated, so alone in the world. You feel you've been used. I sat in front of the fire and sobbed for hours. I wanted my mum more than anyone else.' *35-year-old woman.*

'Somehow I felt guilty because I'd been degraded. I felt unclean, filthy. I thought no man would ever want me again. I didn't want people to see me, and I thought that just by looking at me they would know what had happened.' *Joan B., from Luton.*

'I was so calm – it was as though it hadn't really happened to me. I remember the police telling me they'd never seen anyone so cool and collected. I was even showing sympathy for the rapist, would you believe?' *Pamela, 30, from Plymouth.*

Every woman is an individual, and the way we react to any crisis in our lives varies greatly. Rape is no exception: some women are incredibly calm while others show strong emotional reactions.

There is no way of knowing how you will react when someone grabs you round the neck and forces you to the ground. Many women say if it happened to them they would fight like crazy, but when it's happened they've been unable to scream let alone use any physical resistance. It often comes as a surprise to women that they react so differently to how they had always imagined. Explains Chief Superintendent Sheila Ward, 'By the time we've got over the initial shock of realizing violence is used on us, we've lost the initiative. A woman often freezes up until it's too late for her to try any way of saving herself. Or she is so afraid for her life that she worries any violent move may make the man more angry and brutal.'

For some, the shock and fear is intense yet they find themselves thinking almost rationally. Vanessa, from London, was attacked by a man who pounced with a knife at her throat as she reached her home.

> I can remember thinking, 'this is not happening to me.' The knife was close to my neck all the time, and I was so petrified I could only do what he said. All I could think was I'll let him do this to me and then maybe he won't kill me afterwards. I was quite calm in a way. I remember thinking, 'If he kills me, I hope he doesn't chop me up!'

Most expressed how the shock overtook any other ways they might have tried to get out of a situation: 'More than anything else it's this surprise of sudden contact: imagine how shaken you are when you fall over or trip up a kerb. When someone has deliberately struck you the feeling is a hundred times worse.'

Julie describes those initial feelings when she was raped in her car:

> I was shocked and horrified into a kind of mental paralysis. I was convinced he intended to kill me. I wanted to scream and break free but I was totally unable to do anything but comply with everything he told me to do. I was paralysed with fear and I thought he would kill me. The only way I survived mentally in that hour – which seemed endless – was to try to dissociate my mind from my body just as though it was happening to someone other than me. The only way I could cope with having to be under someone else's will so totally was to 'cut off', so that my mind wasn't really there.

It is often later that the shock hits you. It follows any injury or trauma, and can show itself in many different ways: uncontrollable sobbing, shivering, hysterical laughter, numbness and complete calm, twitching, loss of muscle control.

'After my attacker ran off, I sat down on the stairs and sobbed for hours. I was completely out of control. I'd wet myself too, but only realized this after he'd gone,' says Helen from Kennington.

A woman in this situation needs to be kept warm, and have the support and comfort of a friend.

The effects of shock

Even after the most brutal of rapes, women have often appeared as though nothing has happened in the hours and days after being attacked. The disbelief and shock can have this effect, and the woman can seem to be completely in control of her emotions. Then almost as a delayed reaction, she can become hysterical:

> I was so calm at first, it was all so unreal. I'd expected to die, and yet here I was gathering all my clothes together.
>
> I was staying with my nana at the time, and she's very old and I didn't want to tell her. I tried to act normal, in fact I wasn't even shaking. I went up in the lift to her flat, went straight to the loo, got changed and then went in to see her. She looked at me and said, 'Hello darling,' like she always does, and I completely flipped, and went into absolute hysterics. *Cheryl, from Essex.*

If you've ever seen anyone after a major trauma you'll know the shock may not come until later, or it may not come in the most obvious way of being upset. They can often appear quite calm, almost unaffected by what has happened. They may react by smiling, even laughing – it's the way some people try to control their feelings, by putting what has happened out of their mind. People find that easier to understand as a result of a car crash for example, but to be calm after rape is not so acceptable.

Dr Gillian Mezey, who has spoken with rape victims soon after the attack says: 'I saw a level of control which was almost denial, a total amnesia of the event. One woman actually thought she'd blacked out as she couldn't remember anything, and she was quite cheerful and phlegmatic, going back to work that afternoon inspite of what had happened to her including being quite badly beaten. Another woman remembers talking to a psychiatrist, and says it was as though it had been a friend who had been raped and not herself, as she could not remember any details about when or where it happened.

Jenny, raped by a boyfriend when she was twenty, says now:

> My reaction at the time was to bury it, to behave as if nothing had

> happened. I was afraid of disbelief and being seen to be making a fuss about nothing. I just tried to carry on with life, but found it impossible. I tried to convince myself I hadn't been raped, but I couldn't shake off the effects. I was extremely sensitive to the slightest touch and afraid of men.

Where women have appeared very calm and in control at the time of the attack, three or four weeks later the whole thing hits them. Mixed emotions such as depression, anger, fear, hit the surface.

> I thought I'd coped really well, but suddenly a month after it happened, I was at a coffee break at work and we were laughing and joking about something, then suddenly I was in tears. It was so completely out of character as I hate to make a scene. I've been nervous, miserable and lacking in any confidence since then.
>
> *Heather, from Devon*

There is no set pattern but, where women have tended to be quite calm, to keep it a secret and carry on as normal, they have since said it might have been better had they been able to react immediately.

> At first I didn't want to admit it to anyone, not even myself. The next day I told everyone I'd had a burglary at the house and that's why I was a bit upset. Eventually I became so tense and nervous I had to talk to someone and told a close friend. I had been trying to fight my emotions and my advice to anyone who has to suffer the horror of that deplorable crime is 'Let it out, for God's sake. Don't think you're being calm and controlled by repressing your tears and anger. I remember the police telling me that they'd never seen anyone so cool and collected as me. I was even showing sympathy for the rapist, would you believe? If only I could have broken down and screamed. *Pamela, from Plymouth.*

Susan T, from Bristol, describes how initially she was hysterical:

> I was running round the house screaming, my mum and dad didn't know what had happened to me. Mum was just holding me, and when I told them she called our doctor and he doped me up straight away. I don't know what he gave me but I was on the ceiling, as high as a kite. I think it would have been better if they'd just left me running around screaming because with the drugs I felt so calm, and in fact, bottled everything up for the next few days, and then I went crazy all over again. I think you should be left to cry it out.

Rape is an act of violence during which all control is taken from the woman, her sense of security and autonomy are shattered. A woman who tries to carry on as normal often does so as a way of trying to restore control. She is forced to give in to the demands of someone else, her body being used without her consent. Safety and trust have been destroyed, and victims are often known to revert to a state of dependence, almost childlike.

'I sat in front of the fire and cried when he eventually went. You feel so isolated and alone in the world. You feel so used. I wanted my mum more than anyone else,' said one woman of thirty-five with children of her own, to describe her immediate feelings. Another woman remembers:

> After being at the police station I got home and just felt so flat, I was so tired and just wanted to sleep. I had been crying so much and it was so exhausting at the station that I collapsed into bed. I woke up the next morning and my heart sunk. I eventually moved back home to live with my parents, and clung to my boyfriend much more. I wanted someone to take over my life. I became a recluse for about six weeks and only went out when I had to. I needed to get away from the place where it happened. There was too much to remind me.

There is sometimes a need to move away from the area and the home, particularly when it has been the scene of the crime, but not all women have the financial resources to be able to do so. Sometimes it is also due to fear of retribution by the attacker:

> He lived locally and I'd seen him quite a few times in a pub where I used to work. After I'd reported it, I was so frightened that I might bump into him that I could never be alone indoors or out. Even if someone was with me in the flat, I'd insist we kept the doors locked and bolted twenty-four hours a day.'

Melanie, who was raped in Belgium, felt the same:

> The doctor who treated me out there told me the best thing for me to do was to return home to England. As the police made no effort to keep me there, or persuade me to stay to prosecute, that's what I did. All I wanted to do was put as much distance between myself and Belgium as soon as I could, as I kept thinking my attackers would come and get me again. I think I ran from Belgium as a kind of 'flight' thing.

Mixed emotions

Running away from any problem rarely provides a solution. The nightmares continue, not always of the actual rape, but of something connected with it.

> For nights on end I would wake up to the sound of breaking glass. One night it was so loud I was convinced my window had been broken, but when I looked it was intact. I'd escaped from my attacker by running to a house and banging on the French windows for help. I'm sure my dreams have something to do with that.

Other common reactions are a fear of sleeping in the dark, sudden weight loss or increase, continual headaches, nausea and stomach pain, irregular menstrual cycle, vaginal discharge and severe depression. Women are hit by low moods, uncontrollable crying and sometimes a wish to put an end to it all, another way to 'forget'.

> I was so upset, I just went upstairs and took every pill I could find in the house. I don't know that I wanted to kill myself, I just didn't want to have to think about it anymore. I slept for eighteen hours and when I woke up I felt just the same.

Instead of looking to harm themselves, a more powerful release of their emotions is to feel very angry and want revenge.

> Although I was in a state I wanted to get him for what he had done to me, and I said I'd go round in the police car to all the pubs in the area because I knew he'd been drinking. But we couldn't find him anywhere. While I was feeling angry I felt I was doing something, but when I got home, the shock of what had happened really hit me. I remember lying in bed, shaking at the thought of it – I wanted to sleep and forget about it, but I couldn't as I was terribly tensed up.

Sometimes the anger is expressed against the attacker only, but other times against all men, including those closest to you. 'I hated all men. I'd laugh and joke with them but really I was thinking, "My God, you're pathetic." I didn't give a damn about them.'

It's more likely you'll express anger against all men if the man who rapes you is known to you.

> People have sympathy with women who have been the victims of a violent rape, but what happened affected me just as much. I have lost trust in all men. If a stranger rapes you, perhaps you can still trust the men who are close to you, but when your boyfriend rapes you, who can you trust?
>
> I wanted to get back at men and I did it by acting as though I cared about them, and then dropping them. I think I was trying to show I wasn't beaten, but I ended up feeling even more guilty, out of control.

The message put across by some women is, 'Don't trust men, rape is an act that can be committed by any man, not just this particular man.' You may find this distressing – perhaps you don't see it as an act of man against woman, but as a specific crime.

As such, you look for reassurances by focusing on a certain thing which may have been responsible for the rape – you may say, 'Well if I hadn't been there at that time,' or, 'I shouldn't have hitched a lift.' This can result in the mixed feelings of guilt and self-blame which are bad, but it can help by reassuring you in some way, gaining comfort from knowing that if you alter your actions you won't get raped. It's not necessarily true, but at least it gives you an initial feeling of security. 'This view is often criticized as it can make women feel more to blame,' says Dr Gillian Mezey, who has worked with women at different stages after rape. 'But I've found some victims find it quite therapeutic.'

As an example, Kay says the reaction she had from a friend did not help. 'She said to me afterwards, "You know it hasn't decreased your chances of being raped again, don't you?" What a bloody tactless remark, as I was so scared of it happening again and I still am now, seven years later. It was true, maybe, but deeply disturbing, and it only served to prolong my sleepless nights.'

The guilt and blame seem to come regardless as women search for reasons as to why it happened to them. Did she encourage him by not fighting back? Was it her fault that she was walking in that area late at night? Many women feel they should have done more, or handled the situation in a different way.

> I felt the police seemed to imply later that because I hadn't screamed for help, I had consented. Don't they know what it's like to be so petrified that you can hardly move? Obviously not.

Some research has shown that if you resist you may have a better chance of getting away, but you also run a slightly higher risk of getting seriously injured. As one teenager found out:

> My attacker was quite gentle but I know that if I'd retaliated or tried to scream I wouldn't have got away unharmed. At the court I met two other girls he'd attacked, and one of them had been cut up, with a scar on her leg, yet the other girl had fought like a tiger and she got away. I always thought I should have done more and that it was my fault in a way because I didn't do anything to stop him. But this showed me that there is no right or wrong reaction, and women should not feel guilty. No-one should say they were right or wrong. Only you know how best to respond at the time, and at the end of the day you're the one who has to cope with the consequences of your action.

The consequences are often worse when the attacker is someone known to you. With the stranger-rapist it is easier to think it was all because you just happened to be in the wrong place at the wrong time, and it could have been any woman. But the temptation to feel responsible is greater when the attacker is known to you, and it is often difficult to see it in terms of rape. We are so conditioned by the stereotypes of the stranger-rapist that it is difficult to imagine being forced to have sex by someone you know, in a familiar setting. As a result, women are even more likely to assume responsibility and think they led on the attacker.

Neither does there seem to be so much sympathy: people generally imagine it can't be so bad to be raped by someone known to you, and where violence is not used. These tend not to be seen as 'real' rape, yet the emotional trauma and after-effects are just as great, and often there is less chance of escape; it may be he lives in the same house as you, works with you, and you see him regularly.

Also the belief, by both men and women, that a grown woman cannot be overpowered against her will is false, yet continues in our minds. It takes no account of the paralysing effect of fear in the face of threats or the sight of weapons, and men (husbands and boyfriends) who react by being suspicious and saying the woman didn't appear to do much to get away, can only add to their guilt.

Birmingham Rape Crisis Centre says, 'Relatives and friends

who suggest that the attack was provoked or enjoyed can seriously undermine a woman's recovery, which may take months or years.' Men in particular often find it difficult to understand how fear can paralyse, or that you could not escape in cases where the rapist did not use a weapon. Sheffield Rape Crisis Centre says, 'Women often feel guilty about being raped and feel they could and should have done something to stop it happening. It is not helpful to ask someone why she didn't fight back or run away, or why she accepted a lift with a man she didn't know very well.' It can encourage her to feel that she has been careless or too trusting and that she is in some way to blame. If she is not believed, or thinks she isn't, or you seem to be blaming her, it reinforces the feelings of shame and guilt she already has. One woman says:

> I didn't want to tell him at first. Then when I did, he only added to my guilt by reacting with anger at me! Then came tears and rage, and I ended up apologising, feeling guilty. I'd been sleeping in my own bed, I'd not been walking home late at night, or hitching a lift, even though I know that shouldn't make any difference. Although he never actually said it, I know he blamed me for what happened, because I hadn't screamed or fought back. I was so mixed up myself I can't really blame him for his reactions, but I feel so angry at my own feelings. It's only now, from talking to other women, that I know how common it is to feel that way.

Rape Crisis Centres in Birmingham, Luton and Sheffield already counsel the partners of rape victims, who want to react in the best way, but don't know how to. It is important for those around a victim to be well-informed about how the woman may react and how to cope and deal with certain emotions. It can be confusing for the partner, too, when any efforts to show affection and that he cares, are rejected. It's important not to feel rejected but to understand the cause of such actions, not to give up or to push her into things, but to let her respond to your touches in her own time, and not to treat her 'differently' but be prepared for possible changes in the way that she feels about certain things and what she wants to do, rather than what you think she should do.

It is natural for women to want to cut off from any contact even with those closest to them, and a partner can do much to reassure them of their support and love.

> Somehow I'd been feeling guilty because I'd been degraded. I felt unclean, filthy, I thought no man would ever want me again. I didn't want people to see me, I felt tarnished and dirty, and that just by looking at me they would know what had happened.

So many women have told how the first thing they wanted to do was to scrub themselves 'clean'. Brenda was raped by a man who dragged her into a darkened doorway as she walked home after an evening class. That first night after it happened, she slept in her clothes, not even taking off her mac or her boots.

> I just couldn't bring myself to undress and see my body. I felt dirty and disgusted. I was out of my mind, absolutely distraught. I was terrified of phoning the police because I couldn't face anyone seeing me. The minute I got inside I locked all the doors, pulled all the curtains, and then washed myself all over. I scrubbed my nails, brushed my teeth, I felt dirty, humiliated and totally violated.

One woman, raped in 1967, said how she scrubbed herself with disinfectant: 'I must have made myself so sore, but I felt unclean and defiled, and I was out of my head.'

Helen felt her body was so defiled it wasn't worth protecting:

> Although I wasn't a virgin when I was raped, I'd only slept with three boys and I'd been serious about each of them. I would never consider sleeping with someone unless I thought a lot about them. After I'd been raped, that changed, I just didn't care, my values changed. My mum always said to me, 'You shouldn't sleep with a man unless you love him.' But now that didn't count, I was sleeping with anyone. I think it was also that I was afraid to say 'no' to any man in case it led to violence again.

Other women cannot contemplate the thought of having sex, associating it too closely with the attack, and reject any show of their own sexuality:

> If a man as much as looked at me, I'd freak out completely, I used to walk around looking really scruffy, deliberately playing down my looks. I put on weight, didn't wear make-up. I didn't want to go out with friends, or have any contact with people.

Jenny remembers she could not bear anyone to see her or touch her at all, even a gentle reassuring hug.

> I think it was worse because I had to go to hospital after it happened: they put me in a wheelchair and pushed me through out-patients and I just wanted to hide. I covered my face – I didn't want people to see me. A social worker was left with me. She was sitting there, talking to me, and suddenly I looked down and her hand was on my leg. It was an affectionate gesture but I went berserk. I did not want anyone to touch me. I felt so violated. I wanted my body to myself.

It's not surprising that women find it difficult to resume any kind of sexual contact even with loved ones.

> My relationship with my boyfriend ended. He couldn't bear to see me flinch whenever he tried to kiss me or hold me. I did actually manage to get drunk enough to sleep with him one night, but even that was disastrous. I kept expecting him to turn into a violent maniac and strangle me.

Where women have been able to have sex soon after in a loving relationship, they have all said how much it helped them to overcome their feelings of being worthless:

> Alan insisted in a very gentle way that I told him exactly what had happened to me. I resisted to begin with but eventually I did tell him everything. This helped a great deal. It seemed to make it 'all right' somehow that he still loved me even though I felt so humiliated and degraded. My self-esteem had been taken away, and he helped to restore it a little, but enough to make me feel that I was worth something. He has never made any judgements or made me feel ashamed. We made love the same evening it happened, very lovingly and gently. It was so different from the humiliation and violence of the rape that I have never connected rape with sex with Alan. When I was raped it wasn't what I wanted. It was against my will. But while making love, it's always what I want or it doesn't happen. Thank God I had him, otherwise I doubt if I could have ever had normal sexual relations with a man again.

In those early stages the partner can play a very important part, and it is not an easy one. Some men find it hard to understand that their girlfriend or wife does not want to have sex with them; they will feel rejected, or they may feel confused that she wants to be held and cuddled but is horrified by any kind of more intimate contact.

It is important that the woman is not pressurized into having sex, and it is not unusual, in fact common, for sex, however gentle and caring, to bring back vividly the rape attack. Don't take any rejection of sexual contact personally. Give her time, let her make the decision with your support.

Most of all talk to her: encourage her to talk about what has happened. Many women feel an almost compulsive need to talk about what has happened to them, to get it out of their system, and share it with someone who will not judge them, or find what they have to say unacceptable.

Everyone needs to be able to show their guilt, anger, weakness, or whatever they are feeling without worrying that they will be rejected or blamed, says Birmingham Rape Crisis Centre. They need empathy as distinct from sympathy, trying to understand how they must be feeling, not pity.

> I'm not at all close to my mum and dad and felt really awkward talking to them. I think my dad was embarrassed too. But I've got two elder sisters and one of their friends was terribly raped eighteen months before and, because my sister had sat with her literally for hours after it happened, she understood what I was going through and I found I could talk to her a lot more easily. It's so important to talk to someone who has been through it. I was trying to explain to a friend how I was feeling. But I said, 'No-one understands how I feel.' Then she told me she had also been raped, and it was like a great weight off both our minds. If you can talk about the way you feel, you are sharing the burden of all that's going on in your head. Once I was able to talk it out I stopped having terrible nightmares. *Penny, from Guildford.*

The problem is that the people around you might not want you to talk about it: they might think it's better for you if you don't. They may be unable to cope with it; they may not want to hear. You can feel very isolated after an attack and not talking to you about it can add to the guilt you may be feeling. Rape is treated in a way a bit like the death of a stillborn baby – the less said the better. The stigma attached to rape is still very strong, and one woman said she felt like a leper:

> Friends took a sort of cool, distant approach and that made me feel

even worse, and above all, different from them. I think it's so important to feel that you are not an outcast, and that it does happen to lots of other women so you are not alone. You feel so isolated. Even good friends, especially girls, avoided me. That hurt me most. I know it's because they were embarrassed and it seemed to create this barrier between myself and other people. It made me lonely and increased my anguish. I think some friends were worried that they would harm me more by trying to get me to talk, so they didn't ask the questions they were dying to. I wanted them to ask what was really on their minds. People ask if you're all right, but they don't want to go into detail, and you feel as though you're the only person in the world it's happened to. People just don't talk about it, so you never get to talk to other women about what's happened to them.

If someone close to you is raped it is hard to know what to say to be helpful. But it's enough to say you are concerned, and show love and compassion. Women have said they did not want pity, just someone to talk to them and not treat them as a freak.

I remember one friend sent a card telling me of her love and concern and another just hugged me for a long time, and that helped me enormously. So many women feel alone, discarded, a bit like a pariah, after being raped; you need to know you are surrounded by friends.

Other women talk about the support of family and friends. Where there is no-one to talk to and no support, the attack can turn into a huge secret that is carried around.

I had a close group of friends who I went to school with. The day after the rape they were all sitting in a café bawling their eyes out for me. It's strange, but that helped so much, perhaps knowing that you're not the only one affected by what's happened is a comfort. I had so many people around me: my mum, nan, uncle and friends. *Pam, from Norwich.*

I had a lot of good friends who literally dragged me out the next evening. I didn't want to go, but I think it was the best thing. I'm sure I wouldn't have gone out for months and months otherwise.

Kay, from Surrey

> The fact that my boyfriend was so helpful, loving and supportive: it helped me through that first week. He talked and let me talk, yet some friends tried to smooth it over rather than let me express my feelings. *Maggie, from Kent.*

> When I went back to work, all my friends were very good. The men seemed to have the greatest problems and they seemed different towards me at first: they told me afterwards that they felt so ashamed because they were men too, they didn't know what to say or what to do to try to comfort me.
> *Mandy, from London.*

Dr Gillian Mezey says, 'Most women wanted to talk about it, but some couldn't talk to their husbands because they felt they wanted to protect them. They actually thought it would be too distressing for their husbands to talk about it. So some of them ended up not just thinking of themselves, but also protecting those close to them.'

Where there is no-one within your family or no friends to turn to, the Rape Crisis Centre will always listen to what you have to say. Many of the women who contact them do so within the first week and because they have no-one else to talk to. Some find it easier talking to an anonymous voice at the end of the line. Even if there is not one in your town, you can ring the closest one and they will talk to you and give you advice on medical and legal matters. Said one woman, 'I think Rape Crisis Counsellors should see every woman immediately after they have been assaulted, to explain the feelings you are going through. There should be someone like that with you right from the very beginning.'

A family affair

It is often the case that the whole family needs to be counselled in some way. Rape can lead to a crisis for the whole family. People need to be aware of the way you may react so that they can help you through the initial stages of recovery which are all important.

Victim Support Volunteers have been working recently with rape victims referred to them by the police, particularly in the London area. Traditionally, they have worked with victims of burglary, where maybe two visits are sufficient, but with rape it is very different. However, burglary is an example of how people react differently to crises, explains Kay Coventry of the Victim Support Scheme.

> In a way it can be seen as a more extreme form of burglary. Imagine how you feel when your flat has been burgled, someone has been through your possessions. Well, with rape it is the person who has been violated. While some appear to take it in their stride, others are quite desolate, they want to leave the area, they feel angry, depressed, bitter, have difficulty sleeping at night. Men and women react very differently with burglary; while women show distress, men very often show anger. They are both feeling the same way but they express it very differently. With rape, often the only way men know how to react is with anger.

Two women remember the anger in their family:

> My uncle came over to see me and he said, 'Don't worry, darling, I'll get the bastard, I'll kill him.' My brother, who was just fourteen, grabbed his snooker cue and said he was going out to 'get him' when he saw me arrive home that night all cut up and in a state of shock. As my dad doesn't live with us, I think he felt responsible and thought it was his job to take revenge.
>
> *Mandy, from London.*

> On the night it happened my brother was in bed terribly drunk as they had just had their Christmas Party at work. He told me afterwards that he felt so useless and guilty as he hadn't been able to do anything at the time. I know if he hadn't been drunk he'd have been out there straight away, looking for him. My dad felt bad too: usually he comes to pick me up from work, but this night I walked home as I'd got away earlier than usual.
>
> *Joy, from Swindon.*

The last thing some women want is any expression of anger when they have just been through so much hostility and possible violence. But sometimes it helps to know that the anger is just a cover-up for true feelings of embarrassment and guilt. A mother of a nineteen-year-old who was raped three years ago:

> My husband just could not cope with the fact that our daughter had been raped. He could not accept it and when she refused to go to the police he refused to talk about it at all. I think men do have a lot of problems in the way they cope with crises. Women find it

> easier to scream and cry, whereas men tend to block their emotions: he was so mixed up with his feelings of guilt, embarrassment and trying to come to terms with something so awful happening so close to home. It also affected our sex life too: his guilt and my resentment that men could do such terrible things. We're still trying to pull the family back together. I think more should be said about how those around a victim should react in those early days. You are floundering, as you just don't know what to do for the best.

One woman who was raped also found that her attitude towards her daughter changed. Her twelve-year-old daughter had always been quite an independent child, but suddenly her mother became absolutely petrified for her safety, over-protective towards her, taking her everywhere by car and not allowing her to go out alone. It's not clear whether the daughter knew exactly what had happened to her mother, or whether she thought she had been mugged, but whatever she knew, it must have been very confusing as suddenly her lifestyle and relationship with her mother changed.

It is a natural reaction for parents to become over-protective, when seeing a daughter so helpless: but it is important not to over-estimate their vulnerability.

Particularly where young children are involved, parents often think it is best not to talk about it. Usually, they think that, by not talking, the child may forget, but most children do want to talk. As with adults, this helps them to unburden some of the load, by getting them to talk about nightmares they may have and helping them to feel safe. Children may find it easier to show how they feel in drawings rather than words. Often they don't know which words to use to describe what has happened to them.

> From the age of eleven my uncle made advances towards me, which included heavy petting and using pornographic literature. I did not confide in anyone, my parents had just divorced. My father tried gently coaxing me to talk to him as to my sudden withdrawn moods. How do you put into words what is happening to you?
>
> *Elizabeth.*

Incest can go on for many years, to an age when it can involve the risk of pregnancy in addition to all the other problems.

> When my father found out I was pregnant he stopped, he got scared and left home. In order to protect my family, I said it was my boyfriend, and in a situation when what I needed most was sympathy, I received an endless stream of lectures on contraception and the wrongs of having sex at such a young age.
>
> *Tina.*

A child suddenly becoming withdrawn can be one of the signs that something is wrong. Other signs include being unable to sleep at night, bedwetting, wanting the light on all night, stomach pains, not wanting to go to someone's house or a certain place with someone, being affectionate in a sexual way inappropriate to the child's age, or not wanting to be touched. A lack of trust, not wanting to be alone with a baby-sitter or child-minder, sudden change in school performance and an inability to concentrate, loss of appetite, sadness, running away, thumb-sucking, depression: any parent will know that, taking these characteristics alone, they can be natural, normal responses for a child. But when combined and extreme, they can indicate sexual abuse.

Younger children may be trying to tell of what is happening to them without themselves 'revealing the secret', calling out for the distress to be noticed and acted upon. Many incest survivors have said they were just longing to be asked the right questions.

If a child does talk, usually it will have taken a lot of effort to do so, and needs help to stop it happening. It is most important that you believe what is told to you. Many children said they wouldn't tell anyone if an uncle or other relative made a pass at them, because no-one would believe them. Also because they felt guilty for what had happened. One young girl's father raped her, often violently:

> I used to try to get out of sports lessons, as I had to hide the bruises all down my upper thighs from the other girls and the teacher. I went through a period when I wouldn't talk to my friends – I felt so much older. I always kept my head and eyes downwards. I felt people would simply know by looking into my eyes what was

> happening. I also wouldn't take part in debates in case I opened my mouth and all that my father was doing to me would come pouring out. I don't think I ever felt like a child, so I mixed with older children and was then shunned by kids of my own age.

She needs to know she will be believed and protected, and that she is not to blame. She must be made to realize she is not the only one, and that other children go through similar experiences, so she is not alone.

With all children, after something like this it is important to try to restore their normal pattern of life, yet it can be difficult if the attacker is within the home, and may result in a change of home and school. One of the child's greatest fears is that, by talking, they will split up the family. This is also one of the reasons why women who are raped in marriage endure it and only rebel when the children have left home.

The young girl is often afraid that, if she tells on her father, her mother might disbelieve her or punish her, and she will lose the love of both parents. She may feel anger at the parent who has not done more, feel neglected and abandoned by the mother, which later turns towards anger at the father, and leaves her with the eventual feeling of sadness. It is important for the girl to know her mother is on her side: the father and daughter should not be under the same roof, but *he* is the one who should leave, otherwise the girl will feel *she* is being punished.

Often, just the threat that you – as victim, or someone who knows what is going on – will go to the police, is enough to put a stop to it. Once the secret is out, he will have to stop. Some victims find it difficult to talk to their mother; if this applies to you, try to talk to another female relative or teacher that you are close to, someone who is kind, and who you trust. If one person does not take notice, go to someone else. Or you can talk to someone anonymously who is used to dealing with this situation: the Rape Crisis Centre, or Brook Advisory Centres, or Incest Crisis Line (for all contacts refer to the Resources Section). All calls are treated in confidence and they will not force you to report to the police. If you find out about a case of incest there are different courses of action: seek medical help if necessary; or confidential advice from a self-help group like those mentioned above or Incest Survivors Campaign. Or report to the police, social services, NSPCC, or your GP: the problem will then be taken out of your hands.

Inevitably, once the situation is known, everything happens very fast; often the child has little say in the course of events. Again, like other crises, such as death, there are so many decisions to make, so much contact with authorities: some rape victims have said how everything was taken out of their hands, usually by relatives who wanted to ease the burden, but which in fact only made them feel more helpless. Family and friends can accentuate these feelings of helplessness without really meaning to.

> I can't remember all that happened next, it was all taken out of my hands by neighbours and family. I'm the kind of person who needs to feel in control, but at the time I was in no state to make any decisions.

However, some women welcome it, and when young children are involved there is often no alternative. But as soon as possible the woman should be encouraged to make decisions. Birmingham Rape Crisis Centre says that one of its aims is to help women regain control over their lives by giving support, but not making decisions for her, such as whether or not to report. That must be the woman's decision. Their approach is to give her the information and see how she responds: don't arrange everything, unless she makes it clear she cannot cope; encourage her to start doing things for herself. The difficulty is that many of the decisions and actions that have to be taken *must* be dealt with immediately.

After a death there are details and forms you don't want to have to deal with. After a car crash you have to contact your insurance company and sort out the business of claims. After rape there are tests, possible medical treatment, and deciding whether or not to report.

None can be delayed. We look at reporting rape in the next chapter, not to suggest it can be 'put off', but to acknowledge that not all women feel able to report.

Medical check-up

If you don't have support within friends and family, your local

Rape Crisis Centre can help, not just with emotional advice, but practical things like information on local VD clinics, abortion, pregnancy, female doctors, medical procedures. You may be more badly injured than you think, and if you have any pain or wounds, you should seek immediate treatment by going to the casualty department of your hospital. Even if you do not think you need emergency treatment you should go to your doctor for a check-up: infections such as cystitis, vaginal discharge and itching can be brought on by emotional stress. The possible physical effects are as important as the mental reactions we've already looked at.

In the case of children who have been abused, they may try to conceal the injuries too. Both the hospital and your doctor will ask if you have reported, and your doctor may show reluctance to examine you if he thinks he may be called to give evidence in court. Hospitals may automatically call in the police.

The clinic

The thought of having to have a VD test – when you are already feeling so degraded – is hard to come to terms with, but it is very important to go as quickly as possible in the first week, when most infections can be treated with a course of antibiotics, tablets or injections, as they are easier to treat if detected quickly. Do not think you're all right because you can't spot any symptoms, some sexually-transmitted diseases cannot be detected until a fairly late stage. VD clinics are often within hospitals and known as 'Special Clinics'. You can find your local clinic in the phone book under 'Venereal Diseases', or from your doctor or hospital. You can ask for a woman doctor, though this may not always be possible, and you can take along a friend for support.

The tests that are carried out depend on the kind of attack you suffered, but usually involve an internal examination, swabs taken from the vagina, anus and mouth, along with urine and blood tests. You can go along completely in confidence, and they will not tell your doctor about your visit if you do not want them to. They may ask questions, and if tests proved positive, will ask if you know the name of the man so that they can contact him too. In some cases the woman may know the name of her attacker, but still not wish to give it. If you have had sex with your partner, since the attack, they may also wish to check him. Some results can be given straight away, some take up to a week.

If you were raped you should also consider the possibility that you could be pregnant. Women have said they did not even think about that:

> I had this strange feeling in my head that because there was so much hatred involved, it couldn't happen. I wasn't taking any precautions. This was in 1966 and the pill wasn't freely available, yet I still didn't think a baby would result.

It can and it does. London Rape Crisis Centre say about thirteen per cent of the rapes they deal with result in pregnancies, but the figure could be higher as women often contact the Centre only once. The risk is greater if you were raped about two weeks before your next period is due, as that is the time you ovulate. However, you should *not assume* you are safe just because:

- he did not ejaculate;
- you were taking precautions anyway;
- you haven't started your periods;
- your periods have stopped because of the menopause.

Ejaculation is not necessary, as sperm can be released at any time during which the penis is in the vagina. Precautions are not 100 per cent safe at any time. Rape is no exception, although obviously, there is much less risk if you are protected by taking the Pill or you have an IUD fitted. Also, as you do not bleed until after you first ovulate, it could be you were at the start of your first menstrual cycle, just as the menopause is not always a reliable sign that you are safe from conception. Neither should the fact that you miss a period mean that you are definitely pregnant. The menstrual cycle is often upset by the emotional effect of rape.

There can be other complications: as we've already seen in this chapter, some women found that making love with their partner soon after the rape helped them to diffuse the feelings of worthlessness and not wanting to be touched. But if you have intercourse with your partner just after the attack, but before you have been for your pregnancy test, there could be a question mark over who is the father should the test prove positive. The uncertainty of knowing whether this child is a result of the rape, or from your relationship with your partner, would continue whether or not you went ahead with the pregnancy.

The normal pregnancy tests, free from your doctor or local Family Planning Clinic, cannot be done until one month after possible conception, or fourteen days after a missed period, at which stage immediately go to the Family Planning Clinic, Brook Advisory Centre or your doctor for a free test.

Even if you have not missed a period, a new highly sensitive blood test can detect pregnancy just fourteen days from the time you could have conceived. The result is available by phone the next day. Your local Rape Crisis Centre should be able to let you know if this is available in your area. Chemists and private agencies will also give pregnancy tests and let you know much quicker (often twenty-four hours) but this service is not free.

The do-it-yourself pregnancy tester kits should not be taken alone as a reliable way to detect pregnancy. If the reaction is positive, then you are almost certainly pregnant, but if negative, you still need to have a recheck.

If you cannot wait to have a pregnancy test, you can get morning-after contraception in Britain, which is effective considerably more than just twenty-four hours after the rape. In fact, it *can* be effective up to four days later to prevent a pregnancy. There are two methods, the post-coital pill or the post-coital IUD. However, it is not widely available and attitudes of doctors and clinics vary. Ask them, or consult the Rape Crisis Centre.

If all the tests prove positive, you have then got to make the decision about whether to go ahead with the pregnancy and keep the baby, have it adopted or have an abortion. The sooner you have a test done the better as it will give you much needed time to make your decision. It is one of the hardest decisions to make, and it comes at a time when there is so much other trauma in your life.

> I was doing 'A' levels at the time, intending to study for a degree and aiming for a career. Now I had to face the fears of being pregnant – having a baby was the last thing I wanted. This caused me a lot of anxiety which I kept to myself for two weeks. I wasn't pregnant, but I'd thought so much about what I would do if I had been. The idea of an abortion made me shudder, it still does, but the alternative would have ruined my life.

Some women do not have an alternative: their religion may forbid abortion, or their beliefs may make it impossible to go through with this course of action. They may decide to have it adopted, they may decide to keep the baby. Where a partner is also involved, it can create even more confusion and upset. It is difficult for a partner to understand perhaps that a woman should want to keep a child of the man who raped her. For the woman and her partner it is a constant reminder of the rape.

It is important that you talk it all through with someone, a close friend, or a counsellor. If you decide you wish to terminate you should see your doctor but he may not be sympathetic and may doubt what you have to say, particularly if you have not reported to the police. You could also get help from one of the advisory services; addresses in major cities from the phone book.

Legally, in Britain, you need to have the consent of two doctors and can have an abortion up to twenty-eight weeks, but it is difficult to get it on the National Health Service after sixteen weeks. The time is counted not from the date the rape happened – the date of conception – but from the first day of your last menstrual period, which may add to the number of weeks. Often you cannot afford any delay, and getting an abortion on the National Health Service can take longer than going private. In some cases you may be referred by the Family Planning Clinic or doctor to somewhere like the Pregnancy Advisory Service. Your own doctor may be able to arrange a free NHS abortion, or you may wish to contact a private agency like PAS, where they will be able to talk to you about your problems and feelings. As an example of cost at the Pregnancy Advice Service you can expect a £20 charge for consultation, then the operation can cost from £120-£210 but, as a charity, it is proud of the fact it has never turned anyone away who couldn't pay.

The earlier you decide on an abortion, the less involved the operation is. If you are under twelve weeks pregnant, for example, it can be done under local or general anaesthetic, and you could be out the next day. The Pregnancy Advice Service pioneered the idea of day-care units ten years ago, where you can have an early abortion and return home the same day, and it has since been adopted by the NHS. You could ask the doctor about this.

All these decisions and tests would be difficult at any time but they will be even more harrowing when your emotions are probably in a state of turmoil. People around you must give all the support they can. They will probably feel quite helpless, too, but just knowing they are there will be so important: it is often the strength of others which brings a woman through this difficult time.

5

THE DECISION: Report and Repent?

'How can a woman let a man rape her and not go to the police? My girlfriend would not even tell me who her attacker was, even though she knew him and could have got him sent away. I just can't understand why she didn't tell the police.'

Steve, 24, Bristol.

'However ashamed and distressed you feel, every woman should go to the police – it does take a lot of courage but I knew I had to do it. I'd never have been able to look at my daughter without thinking perhaps she could be his next victim.' *Joyce, 38, Canterbury.*

'Even good friends who had shown lots of sympathy . . . tended to dismiss me . . . I started to feel guilty for not reporting but when it comes down to it, I think only you know whether you are able to report or not.' *Sarah-Jane, 28, Cambridge.*

At a time when you are probably feeling most distraught you have to make an important decision – one that is going to affect you for some time to come. Making up your mind about whether to report to the police is probably the last thing you want to think about.

If your car is stolen or your bag snatched, most of us would call the police without a second thought, but with rape it is not such an automatic reaction. You may find those around you will expect you to do so immediately. Often, the initial decision to report comes from friends and family who take control of the situation and assume they are doing the 'right' thing.

You are not legally compelled to report and the decision to do so should be yours; you are the one who will be most affected. You will make the statement and possibly have to identify the attacker, and go to court – not your friend, or your partner, or anyone else who tries to force a decision on you. If you can't make the decision yourself, talk to other people for advice but don't let them make it for you. You could talk to your local Rape Crisis Centre – their first concern will be for your welfare and, whatever decision you make, it will be respected. If it is someone close to you who has been raped, do not pressure them to report or become 'suspicious' if they do not.

There are many reasons why, as explained further in this chapter, and it takes a lot of courage to decide to go to the police: once they're called in things can get taken out of your hands to a certain extent, as you go through a medical and statement during long hours in the unfamiliar surroundings of the police station, when probably what you most want to do is to go to bed and sleep.

The woman who was the victim in the notorious Glasgow rape case in 1980 (raped and left for dead by her three young attackers) found the courage to bring them to justice and would urge all women to do the same. At the time of the trial she was reported as saying:

> I'd tell other rape victims to try to find the courage to report rapes. I'd say to them, 'Don't hold back, don't be frightened, or ashamed, just go in there and give your evidence, however humiliated, ashamed or dirty you feel. Tell the police as soon as possible. It's not easy but you've got to try. If we don't speak up for ourselves we're always going to to treated this way, as women. We're not supposed to do this or that. We haven't even got the freedom to walk on a street.'

Such words can do more than countless police appeals to get victims to report. The police emphasize the importance of reporting rape as soon as it occurs. Silence, they say, only frees the rapist.

However, it also takes a lot of courage *not* to report – there is bound to be pressure from friends and partners to do so. They will find it hard to understand why you don't want your attacker 'brought to justice', and may start to doubt what 'really' happened.

Two women remember:

> My boyfriend wanted to call the police. I was hysterical at the time and grabbed the phone from him. All I wanted to do was hide under the bedclothes. I didn't want to put myself on view at the police station. I could not face going through it all again, it would have been like reliving the rape. He could not understand why I didn't want to report it, he only saw it as me saying I didn't want the police to catch my attacker, so therefore he decided there had to be something I wasn't telling him. He couldn't understand that I wanted him caught, but I didn't want to have to go to the police.
>
> *Louise.*

> The reaction of friends when I told them I hadn't gone to the police, was that I must have over-reacted and that it couldn't have been as bad as I'd first made out. Even good friends who who shown lots of sympathy and kindness to start with tended to dismiss me and would not talk about it. I'm quite a strong person, but even I started to feel guilty for not reporting. It is *not* the coward's way out, in fact, you need a lot of courage to stand by what you think is right – only you know whether or not you are able to report. *Sarah-Jane, 28, from Cambridge.*

Sarah-Jane is not an exception. Rape is an under-reported crime, and the official figures form only a proportion of the total crimes committed. The Women Against Rape survey found that only one in twelve women reported rape, and one of the main reasons was because they thought the police would be unsympathetic and not believe them. Some felt the police would blame them for being drunk, for hitch-hiking, or because they had invited the man into their home; or they would not be believed because they were too young, a single mum, a student, a punk, not a virgin, on the Pill, black. All these are things which women feel put them outside the accepted photo-fit image of the 'victim'.

Young girls are often put off seeking help if the man involved is someone in authority and/or in their family, as they are afraid of police attitudes, and the possibility of being split from their family, and possibly taken into care.

Other women have little faith in the police and feel reporting would not make much difference.

> I think the thing that really hurts me is that the police could have

guessed what was going to happen. All summer I'd been living at the house, and I'd had several suspicious things happen to me – tampering with the car, funny phone calls, punctures, the sound of prowling outside, and the final straw occurred a month before the rape, when I came back from a night out and found a step ladder up against the bedroom window and my clothes rummaged about in. I had got so scared, I'd said to the police when they'd been searching the house and garden, 'Do I have to get raped before you take notice of me?' I'd been calling them constantly about all these events. Those words still echo in my mind. I didn't stay at the house for a month after that last incident and the rape happened the first night I got back. The only good thing I can say for the police is that they were prompt – they arrived on the scene half a minute after the phone call, perhaps because they'd been in a patrol car at the bottom of the road and had actually asked the man who raped me what he was doing at that time in the morning – to which he replied he was going home after a party – some party!

Bev, Manchester.

Women often don't report because they think it's not worth the trouble; perhaps they're saying they don't think they're worth the trouble and don't want to cause a lot of fuss. Because of the stereotype rapist you may find it difficult to see what happened to you as rape at first. Probably the least reported of all rapes are those that involve a man known to the woman. She may feel she contributed to the attack, or that she will have little credibility because of the situation in which it happened.

I was afraid of police attitudes and disbelief, and of being seen to make a fuss about 'nothing' by friends and family. Because non-violent rapes are not talked about as much as violent rape by a stranger, it leaves the victim with the feeling that it would not be dealt with by the courts, not deemed important. Telling the police was out of the question. They would, I thought, find it amusing that I had been beside a lake, surrounded by trees, in an isolated spot at 11 o'clock at night with him. A situation I was in purely because I trusted my boyfriend. *Jenny, from Brighton.*

Women have expressed similar feelings where they have no physical evidence of the rape, as in bruises or other signs of a violent struggle. The women themselves probably see a 'rape victim' with torn clothes, cuts and bruises and think the police will too. In theory, bruises are not necessary to get a conviction but the response of the police can vary: one woman said, 'I hadn't fought him off at all, but the police didn't ask me why. They just asked if I had and I said, "No, when someone's got a knife to your throat, you don't do you?" and they said I'd done the right thing.' Another woman said, 'Because I hadn't screamed they seemed to imply that I had consented. I said if they'd ever experienced fear like I had they wouldn't need to ask such stupid questions.' A married woman who was raped and beaten was told by the police they didn't believe her story because the assailant was a 'very nice man and would not do anything like that.' They suggested the painful and marked bruising on her groin, breasts and back was due to rough love play, or inflicted by her jealous husband.

There is also fear of reprisals from the attacker, particularly where he had made direct threats and knows where the woman lives. In many cases the woman knows the attacker and may be under constant threat from him. It could be your husband, but only if he used violence could you do anything. Or when the attacker is someone within the family, there is the fear that it would cause the family terrible distress to reveal what is happening. Even when the rapist is a stranger you may also find you don't want to report it, because then all your family would have to know what happened.

> I wanted to keep it a secret from my two teenage daughters as I felt it would affect them badly. Once the police were involved I knew there was no way I could keep it hidden. I wanted to try to forget it myself too, and by ignoring it I thought it might go away and that I could protect my family from knowing. But when I told my boyfriend, he phoned the police. I don't know if I would have done it on my own, because I couldn't face the ordeal. But on a rational level I knew I ought to and I wanted to. I wanted him to be punished and I also felt he would rape again. I would have been conscience-stricken had he raped anyone else.

In some cases, women have welcomed other people making the initial decision to contact the police. As Fiona says:

> I was in hysterics at the time and was saying, 'I don't want the

police.' In fact, I was in no fit state to make a decision really. I'm sure if I had been I probably would have reported it myself. In your mind you feel you've got to help catch this guy otherwise he's going to rape other girls. In the end you don't just do it for yourself but out of a loyalty to all women, and to your family.

At the station

If you decide to report, you should do so as soon as possible, at the police station nearest to where the attack took place (if possible) as this is where the investigations will be carried out. You should not wash, change your clothes, have a stiff drink or take any tranquillizers. It sounds tough on the victim, but by doing any of these things you could be destroying valuable forensic evidence – the medical information which alone could be used to convict your rapist. Vital clues may include a strand of hair, a spot of blood, even a thread from your attacker's clothing.

Women who delay have been accused of needing time to fabricate their story. Police are starting to be more understanding of the trauma rape can cause, and the reasons why we find it difficult to report immediately, but even so, it is important to do so – the earlier you report, the more likely it is a conviction will result.

When you go to the station, take with you a change of clothing, as you will probably be asked to leave your other clothes with them for the forensic department to check for evidence. It is a good idea to have a friend with you for support, as the statement and examination can take a long time – anything from three up to ten hours. However kind and gentle the investigating officers and surgeon, it will be an ordeal to discuss with a stranger what is probably the most traumatic experience of your life.

I was surprised by the kindness of the police after all the things I'd read and heard in the media. I must admit I was pretty apprehensive. Even though the police were kind and sympathetic to me, it was still a harrowing experience. I was questioned by numerous policemen in various rooms and had to repeat my story several times. Although they apologised for having to ask, they did enquire into my past and present sexual experiences, which should not be at all relevant. I finally made a two-hour statement to a

> young policewoman. It makes it much easier to relate exactly what happened to a sympathetic woman. She was with me most of the time at the police station and that did help.
>
> *Louise, from Somerset.*

Louise also had her husband with her at the police station all the time she was there: 'he was just giving me love and support and showing that he cared.'

Turning up with a friend or partner is not always popular with the police as it is sometimes felt the presence of people close to you can make you reluctant to talk about some of the details when making a statement, but they are now more sympathetic to the need for support. If a girl under sixteen is involved then the parent or guardian must give permission for the examination to take place and must be present at the questioning too.

The medical

In the past women have been through lengthy questioning *before* the medical, which has meant they have had to give their statement often in discomfort and grave physical pain because they were not allowed to shower or change their clothing until seen by the police surgeon. In an attempt to ease the ordeal, you will probably be asked to give brief details of what happened; all but the most urgent questions are usually postponed until after the medical. The chances of detecting the offender is found to be only slightly reduced by this delay, and often his identity is not in doubt. Your first contact will probably be with a policewoman who will take the initial details and in most cases will be with you throughout your time at the station. In London these will be specially trained women who will offer support and guidance as soon as you contact the police.

Many women are horrified by the idea of an internal and external examination so soon after they have been raped or sexually assaulted but it is important to gather evidence, such as samples of blood and saliva, which can alone convict a rapist. You can refuse to have an examination but, without it, it is less likely that the prosecution for rape will go ahead. Therefore, the police will try to encourage you to do so because, although they may be sympathetic and believe your story, it would be difficult – if not impossible – to take the case to court. Even if you did not report it for, say, two weeks, it would still be important to have the examination, as it is possible for bruising, for instance, to show up two weeks after.

You can request a female surgeon, or your own doctor if you prefer. But there can be problems: there are very few women trained in forensic evidence and your doctor is not always the best person to do the examination – and of course, she or he may be unwilling. It is far better to have a doctor skilled in rape examination because of the specialist training needed to obtain the forensic evidence and present it in court.

> I think because I hadn't been raped, the police decided that it would be best to go and see my own doctor the next morning instead of waiting to see the police surgeon, which was wrong because I had, in fact, been scratched internally, and later, as a result of this, I got an infection. I don't know why they did that, perhaps they felt it was for my own good so I could get some sleep.
>
> But when I went to see my doctor the next morning and explained what had happened, he examined me but said that I should have seen a police surgeon immediately. He was not prepared to stand as witness in court, so if anything had been drastically wrong, it would not have stood up in court.
>
> *Barbara, from Leeds.*

Police would normally encourage you to see the surgeon and examinations should take place in a proper clinical environment, as detailed in Home Office guidelines; whether this is a hospital, health centre, surgery or police station depends on if immediate treatment is needed, and the facilities available. Police stations are often not the best places. The facilities vary from force to force, as do the surgeons in their approach. In the past there was no shortage of advice for police surgeons along the lines of taking note of eccentricity of dress and use of cosmetics, the way a victim undressed (was she a shy, retiring child or a professional stripper?)! It is inevitable that some of these approaches can still be encountered but, as in all things, there is 'good' and 'bad' and there are many police surgeons who show great sensitivity.

One woman tells of a police surgeon who 'always asks if the

women want a friend present and makes sure the examination takes place in a suitable environment, eg a surgery. He explains he has to try and get as much evidence as he can and then tells her what he is going to do at each stage and asks her, "I now have to do this; may I?"'

However sympathetic, it is still a terrible ordeal:

> I was wheeled to a room in the hospital to be examined. I know they tried to be very sympathetic – the male gynaecologist sat over the other side of the room at first. I knew he was going to examine me. It wasn't the fact he was male, my own doctor is a man, but I did not want *anyone* to touch me at all. I had to spit in some tissues – every one was kept as possible evidence. He said, 'You do realize I have to examine you?' Mentally, I was in great pain, and physically, I thought my bowels were ruined and that I was terribly cut up. I tried to cut off – I was staring at the ceiling and then when he examined me at the back, I clung to the wall. I was in such pain, but I did not want to show it. He said I could shower, but it was too painful – just the water on my body.

The surgeon is looking for evidence of physical force such as cuts and bruising as well as any evidence which could lead to the rapist, such as sperm, saliva or blood, via swabs taken from the vagina, anus and mouth. The victim's clothes are carefully removed, one by one, and later checked meticulously for mud, blood, hair or semen.

> It's the last thing you need at that time, you feel that your body's been violated and now you've got to go through an examination, which is so humiliating, all the swabs stuck everywhere. I tried to 'switch off' and think I was just another body. I felt very embarrassed – I think it would have been less traumatic with a female doctor. He was very good, asked my permission before he did anything and told me exactly what he was doing when he was taking samples, etc. I had to return a week later to have photographs taken of injuries as the bruises were more apparent then. *Cathy, from London.*

Not all surgeons will suggest you return for a follow-up examination, in which case you should mention it as this can be very important as possible evidence if the case should come to court.

Police surgeons sometimes seem to adopt the role of judge and jury, yet their job is to present only an accurate account and honest opinion. They are not required to include information on your past sexual or gynaecological history, yet this is often put into their reports and can be picked up by the defence counsel to your possible disadvantage. The only question he must ask about your sexual background is to establish if you've recently had intercourse apart from the assault, as this could influence the forensic evidence.

Women often think the police medical has also tested them for pregnancy and venereal disease. It has not. Advice on both these tests should always be given. It is not. Some campaign groups believe there should be a central clinic where forensic evidence could be obtained as well as any injuries treated and VD and pregnancy tests carried out, so as to minimize the number of examinations involved.

The statement

After the medical you can ask to go home and rest before giving a detailed statement, although there may be occasions when it is required straight away – for example, if the rapist has already been arrested. Some women feel, and the police may agree, that it is advisable to make the statement as soon as possible while the details of the assault are still vivid. You may find you will go home and just want to forget what has happened, blocking the details from your mind. However, you can insist on giving your statement at home rather than at the police station, although the police point out that you may find it easier talking away from your home environment, particularly if it was where the rape took place, and where you may feel inhibited speaking about it with family and friends present. If you have been raped (or the victim of attempted rape), you can say when making your statement that you do not want your name and addressed disclosed publicly in any proceedings. This should not happen anyway, but it is wise to make your feelings known. You can ask to give your statement to a woman police officer, but this may not always be possible because there are few senior female police officers qualified to deal with such a serious offence. Birmingham Rape Crisis Centre say, in their experience, ninety-nine per cent of women would prefer to talk to a woman police officer, although it is not necessarily true that they will be the most sympathetic: the most important thing is the compassion and understanding shown by the officer, male *or* female. Some say a sensitive man at this stage can be of great value in the recovery of a woman who has just been raped, by restoring some of her trust.

One young woman talks of the kindness shown by a policewoman:

> She was so sweet, and I was crying my eyes out to her. She was cuddling me and saying, 'We'll catch him darling, don't you worry.' Contact and comfort is what you need. It took ages to give the statements because I kept getting upset, and she would say, 'Don't worry, once we've got this bit down, it'll soon be all over with.' She didn't pressurize me into saying what had happened. She explained why she had to ask me each question and I just told her what I could. It all happened just after there was that television programme showing the police interviewing a rape victim and there had been a big outcry over their treatment of her. Perhaps because that had just been shown, they were making a real effort, but I like to think they would have been nice to me anyway.

Special training in some forces, like Thames Valley and the Metropolitan, means you are more likely to come across someone who is specially trained to take a statement from a rape victim, showing sympathy and giving support. Often they will not take notes at first, gently questioning you about what happened.

It can be embarrassing to talk to a female police officer young enough to be your child, or to a man of any age, about intimate sexual details. But try to think of it clinically; nothing you say will shock the police officer taking the statement, as they've probably been involved in similar cases. Often, very intimate questions such as 'Did he put his penis inside you?' 'Did he ejaculate inside you?' will be asked, and you may have to repeat what the attacker said to you. The reason for such questions is that the police have to establish whether rape (penetration of the vagina by a penis), attempted rape, or indecent assault took place. But the officer should do everything possible, by being patient and caring, to make you feel you are not just another 'case'.

Ask any questions you have: the police should do all they can to reassure you and tell you exactly what is going to happen. It is difficult for anyone to go into a police station to report any crime but when it is something as terrible as rape it is bound to be much more difficult. You are talking about your own body to total strangers and, however kind the police officers are, that will be hard for you. You may still find yourself questioned about your sex life even though it is not necessary, apart from when it is said to be relevant to the offence under investigation, for example, about any relationship with the alleged offender. Two women describe their experiences:

> I was annoyed and uptight when they wanted to know about my past sex life, and whether I'd slept with other men. So what if I had? I'm sure it would have gone against me. Even if I'd slept with hundreds of men I don't see it matters to the case, or has anything to do with the fact of whether a man raped you or not.
>
> *Jill, from Bristol.*

> The police came to my house, and a W.P.C. took my statement, from nine o'clock until a quarter to one in the morning. I was very annoyed by some of the questions they asked me, about whether I was a virgin or not, as it was in front of my mum and dad. It had to be because I was under seventeen at the time, but I think they should think of the effect of asking such questions in front of the family. *Debbie, from Essex.*

The only question you must answer about your sex life is whether you have had sexual intercourse in the past week, as this may have relevance to the medical examination (a man's sperm can stay in the vagina for a week or more). A copy of your statement will go to the defence lawyer if your attacker is brought to trial, and the defence may try to bring up any details about your sex life, with the judge's permission, if included in the statement.

You may find it difficult to remember the sequence of events and details such as what was said and the way he spoke. Try hard, as there have been cases where even one word or small observation helped to jail a rapist.

I thought I couldn't remember much, but in fact, I knew quite a

> lot. I remembered him saying he wanted to see me 'nakt'. I didn't know what it meant, but it turned out he was German, spoke quite poor English, and it meant 'naked'. Also, I remembered the unusual handle on the passenger door of his car from which they were able to track him down.

Unfortunately, the police can unintentionally cause you to forget such details, by challenging what you have to say. They have been known to treat victims as suspects when looking for evidence to support what has happened, and often this insensitivity can cause the woman to 'forget' or block out of her mind what has just happened to her and is only able to give the vaguest details. It is a common defence mechanism and can leave you feeling very confused.

Women have described being very distressed and angered by the way in which they've been treated by the police: some say they were met with contempt, insinuations and disbelief.

> The police were not terribly nice to me although I really tried my best to answer all the questions, sensibly and calmly. Half of them seemed to be very disbelieving about the whole thing – partly I think, because I was so controlled and partly because I hadn't screamed. There was a woman police officer there but she was hardly a warm, sympathetic character, and the few that showed me any kindness weren't the ones who took my statement, or escorted me to the doctor.

The police have defended their line of questioning, which in one case went so far as the interviewer shouting at the woman, 'You went with those three boys deliberately, you wanted them to have sex with you.' They had raped her and slashed her with a razor so that she needed over 100 stitches! He explained afterwards that he was 'dress-rehearsing' her for defence questions at the trial. The fact that the prosecution case has to be as strong as possible is often used as an excuse for sceptical police interrogation which leaves the victim with the feeling of being 'on trial': they have said that they need to test the strength of the case, and sort out the genuine cases from the false ones. To test a woman's ability to stand up to cross-examination so soon after the attack can have little significance on how she may react ten months later when the case comes to trial. By then she may be feeling quite a lot stronger. It has been claimed on many occasions that women reporting rape are often lying to cover up something else, such as a young girl who fears she is pregnant, or is late getting home, or is acting out of malice or jealousy. In particular, when there is any delay in reporting, women speak of extra scepticism. Both these assumptions presume that there are women and young girls who would rather go through the ordeal of being interviewed by the police and examined, than face the wrath of an angry partner or parent; and that no woman would delay reporting if she really had been raped.

Luton Rape Crisis Centre says: 'The number of women who report rape for malicious or spiteful reasons is minimal. But we can understand how, when they get to the police station, so many end up by backing down and refusing to make a statement. Once a woman has opened her mouth to the desk sergeant, things start to happen with a vengeance. It is not 'tea and sympathy' and a police car home in about half an hour.'

In any case, it should not be the job of the police to be for or against anyone: when a woman goes into a station to report rape, or any other offence, the police must be totally impartial. It is their duty to record the facts, and once the statement is complete, you should then read it carefully. If you are unsure about something, have it changed before signing each page. You can ask for a copy of the statement at any time up to the day of the trial, but police are not required to give it to you by law, and may be reluctant to do so as the defence could try to bring this up in court to suggest you needed to refresh your memory about what happened!

While still at the station you may have to look through photofiles of known criminals or compile an identikit picture, and you could, at a later date, be called back for the identification parade.

The way forward

Much of the recent police effort to restore women's faith in reporting was started indirectly after a 'fly-on-the-wall' documentary was shown on B.B.C. television in January 1982 showing police interviewing, or rather interrogating, a rape victim. The questioning by four police officers, one a woman, was cynical and very intimate, bringing the woman to tears and confusion. It was put to her that she had been a willing partner and had 'embroidered' her story. No doctor was called to examine her and she eventually withdrew her complaint.

It confirmed women's worse fears about reporting to the police, although it was claimed the woman involved was known to the police and had made false allegations before. Some said it should never have been screened but, as a result, it perhaps made police officers think a little more carefully about their treatment of rape victims and from this developed the first female squad set up in the Thames Valley to deal with offences against women.

The Home Office issued guidelines urging a more sympathetic response from the police, calling for tact and understanding as it was felt women were not reporting incidents. These stressed that it should not be necessary to question a woman about previous sexual experience, except her relationship, if any, with the offender. But as 'guidelines', it was left up to individual forces as to how far they followed them and how much time and effort was put into improving the situation. For them to have any effect they had to filter right down through all the levels. It is impossible as such to say that you'll never end up sitting in a police corridor wrapped in a blanket or come across attitudes that should be outlawed. A Rape Crisis volunteer says, 'I am sure there are sympathetic police officers – in fact, we know there are – but there are still those who see rape as something of a joke.' One referred to rape as 'assault with a friendly weapon'. However, many police forces are working hard to improve things. A Working Party was set up in December 1983 by the Metropolitan Police to look at rape, and was headed by Detective Chief Superintendent Thelma Wagstaff who says, 'We have to make police officers more aware that perhaps we need to be more sympathetic towards victims of sexual offences. If people don't come forward we are never going to stop this crime.'

Already a new, sympathetic approach by the Metropolitan Police has been credited with a huge increase in reported rape cases: in the course of three months in 1985 the number of rapes recorded by Scotland Yard rose by sixty-three per cent.

Deputy Assistant Commissioner Wyn Jones of Scotland Yard's

Crime Department said at the time, 'There may have been shortcomings in the past, but our intention is to improve the lot of victims. We want to kill the myth that rape is sexually motivated – it is usually intended to inflict violence and mutilation, and we want people to report it everytime.'

Ian Blair, a Detective Inspector with the Metropolitan Police Force, has spent much time in the United States studying the way rape victims are treated by the police.

For instance, in New York there is a centralized rape squad, run by women officers, offering the experience and the facilities needed in one place. Some support the idea of setting up a rape squad in Britain just as we have squads for terrorism, drug offences and other serious crimes.

There are plans, in London at least, for Victim Examination Suites – the first opened at the Brentford Police complex in 1986, and it is hoped that this is the first of many: other forces throughout Britain have expressed interest.

In the Metropolitan Police area the aim is for every rape/sexual assault victim to have the benefit of the facilities of these Suites where there will be specially trained officers with instructions to allow women to rest and recover before detailed questioning, and the provision of showers and overalls for after the medical. There are plans to have more female surgeons on call as well.

Special training courses are held at Hendon for police officers and Detective Inspectors to learn about rape and its effects so that eventually the Metropolitan Force will have a team of specially trained D.I.s backed up by male and female officers who are familiar with rape trauma.

Ian Blair also stressed this need in his book *Investigating Rape* (Croom Helm, 1985): that a change in police rules is not enough without a change in basic police attitude. It is vital that, as it may be the first contact a rape victim makes with anyone after the attack, the police understand what she is going through, by learning more about rape trauma. For example, it might be expected that a rape victim would appear distraught but, equally, there are many who are in a state of shock and may appear almost unconcerned at the time – almost as if they were reporting a stolen bicycle! Two weeks later these same women may be in need of psychiatric treatment, so it is obvious there is a great need for more awareness of the on-going support they may require.

The more the police know of the emotional problems of rape, the better able they will be to help you. They should give advice on medical, social or voluntary help that is available, and the officer should keep in touch to let you know exactly what is going on.

Compensation

The police should tell you about the possibility of applying for compensation as a result of rape or sexual assault through the Criminal Injuries Compensation Board. In the Women Against Rape survey, half of the respondents had never heard of the CICB, and there was no greater awareness among women who had reported a rape or sexual assault to the police, so it is evident that women are not being told. The CICB is a state body which makes payments to victims of violent crime in Great Britain. Some do not realize they can apply for compensation for rape or sexual assault: and in theory, it is not essential that you have reported to the police. But because independent evidence is needed, it is far less likely an award would be made. There can be a lot of expense and suffering as a result of rape and although you may, quite rightly, say money cannot begin to compensate for being raped – you may even find it distasteful to think of what has happened in monetary terms – it can help ease the burden in practical terms for wages lost during recovery. Also taking extra precautions such as fitting extra locks, running a car, moving home, and paying someone to care for your children as you may feel unable to cope with their demands and the attention they need, to medical expenses such as the cost of a private abortion resulting from the rape.

While these costs are covered, the expense of raising a child resulting from rape is excluded. Some women may choose to have an abortion but for some it is not an option (it may be too late, or it may be against their beliefs). It is hard enough to accept a child in these circumstances but the decision should not be influenced by whether you can afford to support the child. Rape Crisis Centres believe this should be included in the compensation.

Get someone to help you fill in the form, perhaps someone

from a Rape Crisis Centre, or a police officer. You should include all the details from obvious financial ones to emotional and mental stress it may have had on your life, such as splitting up with a boyfriend, fear of going out, sleeplessness. None of these is too insignificant. Birmingham Rape Crisis has already helped several women with applications and some of these were awarded substantial amounts on the basis of their suffering and shock, even though they had not been physically injured or absent from work.

The compensation does not depend on a verdict in court and, although you may not hear anything for up to six months, the Board would not necessarily wait for the outcome of any trial. However, you should apply as soon as possible and it *must* be within three years. Delay will be considered in any award made and has been known to lead to a reduction. It may also be withheld or reduced if you have not taken, with delay, all reasonable steps to inform the police and bring your attacker to justice, or if there was any responsibility on your part through provocation or otherwise. The award is discretionary so as such you may hear no award has been made, or you will be told how much. The CICB does not publish recommended amounts, but the average payout for rape victims is in the region of £3,000 (1985 figures). It can be more, it can be less. Compared to the five figure amounts often given to people in car accidents who have perhaps lost all sexual feelings, it is minimal. How women feel about sex after rape is not generally reflected in rape compensation, yet is a common long-term effect.

If you do not feel you have been awarded enough, you can appeal, in which case you will have to attend a private hearing where the board (usually three people) will cross-examine you and any witnesses to both the crime and to your state afterwards, as well as looking at any other evidence and medical reports submitted. A decision is made on the spot, and is final. It could be that they lower the award: do consider this when thinking about appealing.

Apart from advice on compensation, there are very many other areas where the *combined* support and advice of police and agencies such as Rape Crisis should be used to help women in this situation. But it is not always available. One reason is the limit to the amount of time police can give in terms of follow-up and help, and in most cases they lack the specialist experience of Rape Crisis for example. In some areas a good relationship has been established between the two, such as in the Midlands where Birmingham Rape Crisis has contributed to the training of police officers in the West Midlands and Staffordshire forces. In London a victim may well be referred to the Victim Support Scheme instead. This scheme is more usually concerned with crimes such as burglary but has recently started training its volunteers to cope with rape/sexual assault and violence. However, its work is strictly limited to cases referred by the police, whereas the Rape Crisis Centre has an essential role for *all* women, including those who don't want to report and wish to remain anonymous. It refuses to encourage woman to contact the police.

At the end of the day it is YOU who is the important person and, whatever your decision about reporting, the voluntary agencies and/or the authorities should do all they can to support you.

6

THE JUDGEMENT: Witness for the Prosecution

'Before it happened to me I'd sometimes hear women say they wouldn't take their attacker to court, and I used to think, "My God, how stupid!" But now I can understand it. You go through so much and then he walks out of the door with you. It is the thought of the injustice that grates so much. It was like a slap in the face, knowing that he walked out of that court a free man.'

Louise M., 22, from Birmingham.

'I felt as though I was an exhibit in court, with all those strangers piling into the public gallery. At one point when I was being asked questions it was as though it was I who was the one on trial and was going to be given a sentence to serve.' *Ruth, from Norwich.*

'Having him put away gave some satisfaction – it wasn't the revenge aspect of it but it was just like having the rest of the world supporting me. The relief of a higher authority finding him guilty made me feel good. You think no-one believes you till you hear that "guilty" verdict,' *Theresa, from Liverpool.*

Waiting for the day you hear the police have caught the man who attacked you may be long and distressing . . . it may never arrive. Reporting the offence does not guarantee a case will be brought against your attacker, and neither does taking him to court guarantee a prison sentence. In 1983 of 1,334 rapes reported to police in England and Wales only 310 resulted in conviction.

The progression from giving evidence to the police and going to court seems to have little concern for the victims. At this stage you may feel quite helpless, dependent on others. It does not help that you are left in the dark, not knowing what to expect, and not understanding the judicial process. Once a complaint has been made in Britain (except Scotland) it is first up to the police whether they investigate further, and then the police and the Director of Public Prosecutions whether to prosecute and what charges should be brought. In most other countries (including Scotland) some or all of these functions are performed by independent officials, such as investigating magistrates or the Office of the Procurator Fiscal (whom the woman may contact during the preparation of the prosecution).

It is not surprising to feel distraught if you suddenly hear, without any explanation, the case may be dropped. For example, this may happen if a young child is involved and the defendant pleads 'not guilty', because it is often felt it could be too traumatic and damaging to the child to go to court. Or you may learn charges are to be brought for a lesser offence than rape, or that the attacker cannot be brought to trial because of lack of corroborative evidence. It may make you feel you have not been believed.

You should be kept informed of each stage of the legal process for which the utmost sensitivity and care are needed, but are not always shown.

'The police officer said to me once they'd caught him that, without wanting to appear facetious, it now had little to do with me and he'd get back to me when he needed more information.' It is often the case that once you leave the station you do not know what will happen next; it is not usually made so explicit.

However, you may hear nothing for months and then suddenly get a call 'out of the blue' from the police asking you to attend an Identification Parade as they think they've found the man who attacked you. The thought of possibly coming face to face with him again can be terrifying; some women had to do this soon after making the statement, for others it was a lot later. One girl remembers:

The worst part was the ID parade: to be faced with a whole line of

> strange men, knowing he could be among them. The night before I was terrified, as I could not recall his face at all. I was sure I wouldn't be able to recognize him. The police wanted me to take my time. I think they were pretty sure about the man, but I couldn't say for certain.

There will be police in the room while you walk along the line-up who will tell you that there may be someone who attacked you in the line-up but there may not be.

> I suppose like other women I had thought 'Oh God, what if I don't recognize him,' but I saw him as soon as I walked into the room. There were about twenty men in the line-up and because my attacker had a broken nose, they all had to have plaster over their noses. I saw him the minute I walked in: all the others were looking at me, apart from him. His eyes were looking down. It was a horrible experience to have to face him again, but at least I knew they'd got him.

Police forces are looking at the American idea of one-way mirrors for identification parades, to afford the victim more protection. Strathclyde already has this, and other forces are looking at the idea.

The long wait

It does come as a shock to most women to find that the crime of rape is a crime against the State, and that they, the victim, are treated as a witness to the crime (the same applies to other crimes, even attempted murder). The prosecution is not brought by you but by the State, so you will be called to court as chief prosecution witness to give evidence; you will be cross-examined and then told you can go. As it is the police who decide whether or not to prosecute, the full costs of bringing the case are paid out of public funds.

The prosecution solicitor and barrister are appointed by the Director of Public Prosecution (as such you have no direct legal representation) and it's unlikely you will have any contact with the solicitor until you turn up at court. The case rests effectively on your statement of what happened, which you may not have seen since you made it many months ago, and some argue the victim should receive counsel, as does the accused.

Rape Crisis Centres believe you should be given more power to bring your own prosecution if you choose, and to instruct the solicitor, so that you have greater control over the course of the investigation and the proceedings of the trial.

The legal process can take months to complete, during which time you may know little of what is going on, unless the police officer involved in your case cares enough to keep you informed. He/she is probably the only contact you have, and should realize that, having been subjected to questions and a medical examination, it can add to the trauma you have already been through if you are given no further information.

It is a very difficult time – knowing that at any moment you could be called to court. It is a constant reminder which hangs over you, and women have said how difficult it is to try to come to terms or 'forget' what has happened when you know you may be called to 're-live' it in the courtroom.

'It is the not knowing that cracks you up,' says one woman who finally refused to give evidence as she wanted to put the experience behind her once and for all. Another described the long wait:

> You go through days and months just waiting. I had so much time to think it over, that I started to have second thoughts about going through with it all. I phoned the police twice about withdrawing my statement, but they said they had a strong case against him. I was so afraid of going into court to give my story and perhaps be called a liar. I was absolutely terrified about giving evidence, I knew I had to do it but I was frightened they were going to crucify me in court. I was so tired of the whole thing. I didn't really care what happened to him but I went through with it – almost out of loyalty to the police and my family.

This is a common reaction – women are often expected to feel vindictive and revengeful when their attacker is at last sent to jail but for most it is more likely they will feel weary, 'drained', and go along with the proceedings because they feel it is the right thing to do.

If you really cannot go through with giving the evidence and wish to withdraw your statement, the police may try to persuade you not to, but eventually, as you are chief prosecution witness, they may have to agree not to proceed. You will have to sign a formal withdrawal document. However, if your attacker is held in police custody, it is more complicated – the police would be *very* reluctant to drop the case and the decision would have to be made by the Director of Public Prosecutions.

Mandy, from Oxford, was fortunate in that she was kept informed:

> It took about a year and half in all from the day I was raped till when it came to trial; the court procedures do draw out the suffering. I desperately wanted to get it all over very quickly so I could start to forget, but I think I was luckier than most in that the police were very good and kept me in touch with what was going on. There was this enormous detective with ginger hair and he was caring, and sweet to me, telling me what was going on.

Dr Gillian Mezey, who has interviewed many rape victims, believes some of the distress is because they cannot remember exactly what happened, or what the attacker looks like:

> It is very difficult for women because of the long space of time before it comes to court. Many of them try to forget, deliberately to start with, and then suddenly they are called to court to give evidence.
>
> One particular girl was certainly distressed at going to court as she felt she wouldn't recognize the man, and that she'd actually have to say something about him in court and commit perjury because she could not remember. She'd built up this nice little cocoon around herself in which she'd convinced herself nothing had really happened. Now here was this fear of being faced with her attacker, and all the defences she had built up would break down.

'Proceed' with care

The more informed you are, the better able you will be to cope when the case comes to court. Victim Support Volunteers and Rape Crisis Councellors can usually provide you with information as well as giving you emotional support. VS Volunteers in particular liaise with the police, finding out from the station exactly what is happening, and what stage the investigation is at. Of course, you can do this yourself, but it is often best to let someone who knows the procedures find out for you, as they are often lengthy and complicated.

Rape is an indictable offence, which means it is tried by judge and jury at a Crown Court. But before that happens, there is an initial hearing at the Magistrate's Court (offences involving indecent assault are dealt with here in their entirety) which is known as the Committal and happens soon after the police arrest. At some of the new style Committals the statements are read out and it is not necessary for you to attend. However, sometimes the prosecution or the defence request a special 'old-style' hearing. The prosecution often ask for this if they have doubts about the woman's ability to give evidence, or the defence if they think there is insufficient evidence. The magistrates consider whether the case should be sent to trial, and you can be called to give your evidence and be cross-examined.

A lot is written about the police powers to drop cases, but even if they think there is a strong case and decide to press charges, the magistrates have the power to dismiss the charge at this stage if they think there is not enough evidence. The case will come to a halt and you have no right of appeal.

However, it is possible in Scotland, through a loophole in the law, for an individual to bring a private prosecution with the Crown's consent, as was shown in the case of a Glasgow woman who was raped and left for dead by teenage attackers in October 1980. As a result, she needed 168 stitches, and had tried to commit suicide. It did not help when she read in the newspapers that her case had been dropped, as Scottish legal officials had decided not to prosecute her attackers in case the stress of taking the witness stand damaged her health still further. So she brought her own case – the first successful prosecution since 1909 – and it led to substantial reforms in the legal system of Scotland. No rape or murder prosecution can now be dropped without the Lord Advocate's consent, and the Crown has accepted that all crime victims have the 'right to be told' if charges are going to be dropped.

Women believe they have the 'right to be told' if their assailant is bailed, but there have been cases where the woman does not know until she sees him for herself.

At the committal stage the man is charged and is usually remanded in police custody until the trial if the charge is rape. His defence can apply for bail which can be opposed if it is shown that he might interfere with the witness, commit further offences, or not turn up at the court. Although there are no statistics to show how many rapists are bailed before trial, some most certainly are. 'Remanded on bail' means released with certain conditions, such as reporting each day to the police station or keeping away from the victim.

To find out that the man who attacked you is walking the streets is the last thing you want to know, particularly if he made some kind of threat to you at the time of the rape about not reporting. There was an attack on a twenty-one-year-old university student as she walked home after studying late. She says: 'After attacking me he insisted on walking me home, so he knew where I lived. I was horrified when I heard he'd been let out on bail, and I was terrified to be left alone in the house in case he came for me again.' Any such threats can be used as evidence to show he should be remanded in custody, but this does not always happen.

The man who was charged with indecently assaulting Debbie T. was put on a curfew, which meant he was not allowed out after seven o'clock at night.

> But he was seen breaking it. The police said unless they caught him there was not a lot they could do. My dad was furious and he rang up the police and said he was sick and disgusted at the way his daughter was at home a nervous wreck and *he* was walking around on bail.
> *Debbie T.*

The courtroom

The time between the Committal and the Crown Court hearing can be anything from six months to a year, plenty of time to sit and worry about what it will be like in court. Most people have not been in a courtroom before and the experience can be awesome. Kay Coventry of the National Association of Victim Support Schemes says they suggest a woman may wish to go along to the courtroom with a volunteer when it is empty so she can see what it looks like, and where everyone sits. Other women have even chosen to watch a case in progress from the public gallery:

> A friend of a friend worked as a shorthand reporter at the Crown Court and she suggested it might help me to see exactly what happens. The first day was awful, I saw this woman break down when she was being questioned, and I thought, 'My God, that could be me, I can't go through with it.' I made myself go back the next day. She was still in the witness box and she was so brave, denying everything that was put to her. It gave me courage – you see another woman going through it and it makes you think, 'I've got to do it too' – the alternative is that women will never be safe.
>
> *Susan S., 23, from East London.*

Some women cope with the long wait by putting it to the back of their mind – the idea of going along to see a case in progress would force them to face up to it, as Michelle F. explains:

> The Crown Court was like a no-go area of the town. If I was out shopping I'd deliberately go round the long way to avoid walking past it. I've always coped with bad things in my life by not thinking about them, and I suppose that was what I was doing. When it came to the day I had to go to court I was absolutely terrified. I find anything to do with authority terrifying – all these people with wigs and cloaks walk in – I had no idea what to expect. Perhaps if I'd been more familiar with it all, I might not have been so frightened.

Familiarity is good for most things: when you don't know what to expect, anything can be daunting. Think of when you start a new job, and you're going into a strange office with lots of new faces. By the end of your first week everything seems more friendly and pleasant.

It would be stretching the imagination too far to say the courtroom is pleasant. Often, the only people you will know are the police officer dealing with your case and the assailant. The judge usually sits at a table on an elevated area like a stage where he listens to the proceedings, makes the odd interruption and takes his own notes which he may use in the summing up. Opposite the judge, on the other side of the room, is the dock where the assailant will sit, usually with a guard. On one side of the courtroom is the jury, twelve people, chosen from the electoral register, facing the area where the barristers (in black gowns and white wigs), solicitors and clerks sit – and the police officer connected with your case. There is also a shorthand writer who takes down everything said in court, and an area for the press. The Crown Court is usually open to the public, who can watch from the public gallery overlooking the court (or a small area at the back in the Magistrate's Court). The witness box is usually situated between judge and jury, and this is where you will be called to give your evidence and be cross-examined.

If the defendant (your attacker) pleads guilty you do not have to go into the witness box or attend the trial. If you wish, you can still be present but you will most likely have to sit in the public gallery. In some cases he may plead 'not guilty' to start with (which involves you giving evidence) but may change his plea to guilty on the advice of his solicitor as often a lesser sentence is likely because it shows (or appears to show) some compassion on the part of the assailant if he saves his victim from the ordeal of going into the witness box, and also a judge and jury may be influenced by seeing the woman giving evidence.

Some women want to give evidence to show how much effect it has had on them:

> I had to sit in the spectators' gallery and watch as they led him out of the cells into the court. Then they read out what happened, just as though it was a report, the facts but nothing of the emotion and fear. I was sitting there thinking, 'My God, this is not how it happened. This is not how I felt or how he looked that night.' I had to listen to all these people saying what a good man he was and how he did community work and helped local people, and how his girlfriend and parents were standing by him. I wanted to speak too, to say how it had been on that night and how it had changed my life. But because he had pleaded guilty, I couldn't say anything – he was probably advised that it would be better for him if I couldn't give my evidence. *Mandy, from London.*

> The policewoman even told me not to go to court and sit in the public gallery. I wanted to go so that people would realize what he had done to me. But I think the police thought I wouldn't be able to control myself, as I'd had a few words with them already. I've since heard that solicitors often advise their clients to plead guilty

> because the sight of the victim in the witness box turns judge and jury. It's completely different when they just sit there and listen to reports read out to them. *Linda, from Nottingham.*

Summoned – witness for the prosecution

If you are called to give evidence you will receive notice of the hearing and a summons to appear in court, often only a few days before the case is set to start. You must attend unless you are ill (in which case you will have to supply a medical certificate). If you do not turn up without giving a reason, a judge can order your arrest to bring you before the court.

It is a good idea to go with someone: if you do not have a close friend to rely on, you could always contact your local Rape Crisis Centre who would go with you if it is what you want. It's unlikely there will be anyone to meet you at court and tell you where to go, so it helps to have someone who knows what you should do and where you should go when you arrive. Some women have been shocked to find themselves waiting in the same areas as the accused's family, and in some cases the accused himself! You could find yourself waiting to give evidence next to the attacker's wife or girlfriend. If he has been on bail, it is quite possible you could come face to face with him at the court, before the trial has even started. Rape Crisis workers in Birmingham try to find out exactly what time a hearing will start so that they can turn up with the woman just before the hearing, to avoid unnecessary waiting.

Some courts where space permits, try to arrange a room or small area where the chief prosecution witness can wait away from the defendant's family. If the defendant is in custody, you will not see him until he is brought into the dock (if you are watching from the gallery) or when you go in to give your evidence. By this time, the jury will be in their seats, and the accused in the dock. This is probably the first time you have seen the man for months, and can be very frightening, particularly if he made threats to you. It can be upsetting too if the man is someone you know quite well. He remains in the court all the time you are giving evidence and being cross-examined, which adds to the ordeal:

> To walk into that courtroom and give evidence was the most

> difficult thing I've ever done. As I walked past him I kept my head down, I knew I couldn't look at him. He had been committed on forensic evidence, so I hadn't had to identify him. I couldn't picture his face and I wanted it to stay that way. I'm sure his face would have been with me always otherwise, like a ghost hanging around, for the rest of my life.

The family and friends of the defendant may also be watching from the public gallery which can make it even more harrowing:

> The defence was saying that I'd agreed to sex and that I'd enjoyed it. All the time I was stared at from the dock by the man who did this to me, and in the gallery there was his wife and mother giving me filthy looks. Rape is a humiliating experience forced on you; going to court isn't so very different. How low do they want to make you feel? If going through that is not victimization, I don't know what is?

Another woman comments:

> A friend of his was in the public gallery and she actually shouted out 'She's a con' and other abuse before the judge warned her. I thought, right, I'm not going to cry in front of her. I wasn't going to let myself down in front of her. I could feel her glaring at me the whole time, but in a strange way it helped, because I was concentrating on my hatred of her more than anything else.

The gallery and courtroom is only cleared at the discretion of the judge in certain circumstances, such as cases involving a child. Many women fear the possible publicity going to court may involve. Even in rape cases, your name and address can be read out in open court in the hearing of the public gallery where his friends and family may be, unless you request otherwise to the officer in charge of the case. You can make a similar request if the charge is sexual assault but in this instance there is no guarantee your wishes will be granted.

Since the Sexual Offences (Amendment) Act 1976 victims of rape and attempted rape are given protection by the courts in so far as press, radio or television can report the case but must not publish the name and address of the victim or any details which may identify her. Victims of indecent assault do not have the same rights: any description of you or your life is allowed, as well as your name and address. Some believe the anonymity given to rape victims should be extended to indecent assault.

In all cases, the courts prohibit the publication of any details which could lead to the identity of any child or young person under seventeen. However, unless the court makes a special order, the offender's name, once convicted, can be published and, in incest cases for example, this could lead to the identity of the victim.

Defendants in rape cases have the right of anonymity, and can only be identified if found guilty. This is not the case with other offences and there have been recommendations to abolish it for rape. The problem with doing this is that by identifying defendants in rape cases it could lead to the identity of the woman being disclosed, particularly as so many cases involve men known to the victim. The alternative is that other offences should be made to fall in line and all defendants in court given anonymity until conviction.

In exceptional circumstances a request can be made to lift reporting restrictions. This happened during the Hutchinson Murder Trial in 1984: the young girl who was raped by the man who had just killed her parents and brother, became the first rape victim to be named in the newspapers, on television, and radio since 1976. It was felt that the offences of murder and rape were so inextricably linked that reporting restrictions should be lifted. But it caused untold suffering for the witness, particularly as the Press showed so little sensitivity in reporting the trial.

In the box

From the witness stand you will be taken through your statement by the prosecution barrister. Although it's likely you have not met him before, he is bringing the case against the accused (which means he is on your side). You may see your statement shortly before the proceedings start, which may help as it's likely you have not seen it for months. Also, it was made at a time when you were probably very distressed, so it could well be unfamiliar to you, and you may find it difficult to remember what you said. Even after many requests the police may be reluctant to give you a copy of your statement as the defence often suggests the woman needs it to 'refresh' her memory, and tries to cast doubt on her credibility as a witness to the events.

The defence will then cross-examine you, challenging your story and looking at what happened from the assailant's statement, which will conflict with yours. Try to remain calm. He is trying to confuse you, undermine any confidence you may have or to get you so annoyed that perhaps you will appear uncertain of events and over-defensive, thereby casting a slur on your character, intelligence and credibility, and making you out to be an unreliable witness.

> All along I was frightened of giving evidence because I know when you stand in that box they throw all kinds of questions at you and try to make you look like mud! You are treated as though you're an exhibit. Mum said I should try to keep calm, take my time answering the questions and I'd be all right. My doctor said she would put me on tranquillizers for a couple of days, to keep me calm, but I said no, because I thought it might slow down my reactions and make me seem unsure. *Christine, from York.*

All your replies should be directed through the judge, and you are not allowed to speak unless asked a question, so you can end up feeling insignificant. The judge may hardly look at you, and the feeling that you're being talked about, rather than talked to, is not unusual.

Once you've given your evidence and been cross-examined (this can often take a whole day or more), the prosecution can ask for you to be released as a witness, which means you can leave the court. As long as the defence agrees, this usually happens, but with the proviso that you should be available if called upon during the rest of the trial. Some women want to sit through the whole trial which may involve other witnesses, a neighbour, for example, giving evidence to verify your state after the attack, or the police doctor (the medical report may be read out in court instead of a doctor attending) and other evidence like a follow-up medical report on the long term emotional and physical effects. Then the defence case follows, where the assailant takes the witness stand, and other defence witnesses may testify, such as to his character. The prosecution then sums up followed by the defence. Some women stay through all this — it can often last three days or more — as they want to know exactly what goes on and what is said, rather than just hearing the outcome. The prosecution may discourage you from sitting through the remainder of the trial as it may cause the jury to have doubts over your motives for doing so, and think it has had little effect on you. However, there should be a separate area for women to sit at the back of the court, rather than listening to the remainder of the trial (if you wish) from the public gallery. Birmingham Rape Crisis Centre has an agreement with the city's Crown Court that if they attend a case with a woman they can sit with her in the 'well' of the court as opposed to the public gallery.

Most women do seem to get away as quickly as possible:

> I hated the courtroom, I just had to escape. I really did feel as though I was the one on trial, you go through so much, all those awful questions. If I'd had to stay there for much longer I would have been physically sick.
>
> Going into court to give evidence on anything is a frightening experience but when it is something so personal it is much, much worse. *Lyn, from Newcastle.*

The burden of proof

The basis of British justice is that a person is innocent until proven guilty. Therefore, in a rape case as in any other, it is for you (the prosecution) to prove the accused's guilt. He need say nothing in practice; yet the defence will challenge your evidence. Once in court rape is treated in a peculiar way: in no other crime is such a blameless character and conduct called for on the part of the victim. For example a woman carrying a purse is not generally considered to be asking to be mugged, but a woman in a short skirt is often accused of asking to be raped. In the event of a bank robbery the 'victim' (e.g. the bank manager) is not asked what he may have done to provoke the crime.

But in rape the defence try to allege that the victim willingly allowed herself to get into the kind of situation that a 'sensible' woman would have avoided, so in a sense she is held responsible for the rape.

Blame is attributed to women who are seen to put themselves in vulnerable situations, but which are, in fact, situations in which any woman might find herself. Ask yourself if you've ever slept with your window open at night or have ever gone to the front door with your dressing gown on? Or walked home when you haven't had the money to take a taxi? If you answer yes to just one of these, had you then been raped you could have found people saying to you in court that you 'asked for it' by making yourself open and vulnerable. There was a case of a woman who slept naked in a basement flat. A man broke in and raped her, and because she was naked she was seen to have provoked the crime. The moral of this story: respectable women do not sleep naked in bed!

It's easy to make a joke of it. It would all be quite ridiculous, and laughable, if it wasn't so tragic and true. Sadly, it isn't unusual to hear such allegations in British courts.

> There was one point, when I was being asked questions, that everything in court seemed unreal, as though I had walked into a farce. I actually felt that any minute I was going to be given a sentence to serve and dragged down to the cells screaming. They can make you feel so guilty. If you don't laugh I think you'd cry. The thing is, if it looks to the jury as though you're treating it all too lightly, or trying to be clever to outwit the defence barrister, chances are you'll lose any sympathy they may have had for you.
>
> *Elaine, 56, from Swansea.*

How you stand up to the pressures of the witness box has a lot to do with your character. While some women become heated and aggressive, others are reduced to tears by the harsh questioning of the defence:

> I'd been absolutely terrified all along of going into the witness box. I hate being the centre of attention even at a birthday party, but here I was supposed to make public all these terrible things that had happened to me. In my mind I was singing a song, so I wouldn't have to hear all the details. I can't remember much of it now, it was eighteen months ago, and I've tried to block it out of my mind. I can remember my knees knocking and I must have looked pale because they said to sit down and they got me a glass of water. I was frightened of getting all tied up in knots when they

asked me things, and to make it worse you've got all these people watching you, making their own decisions about whether you're telling the truth or not. *Judy, from Liverpool.*

It comes as a surprise to many women who have been through the courts in the last ten years, that in 1976 the Sexual Offences (Amendment) Act was introduced to prevent rape victims being put 'on trial'.

It was designed to encourage more women to come forward and report, by promising rape victims the fullest protection when giving evidence in court, and in particular to shield them from intense cross examination about their sexual past. Up until then rape victims were questioned about any aspect of relationships with men, seeking to discredit a woman by highlighting any facts which they thought would cast some slur on her character such as the fact that she had had an abortion, she was a prostitute, or that she had an illegitimate child. As a result of a public outcry the Act placed restrictions on bringing a woman's past sexual history into court (it was left to the discretion of the judge) and confined questions on a woman's sex life to the relationship, if any, with the man or men on trial. In spite of the restrictions judges frequently give leave to the defence to bring in evidence about the woman's 'past sexual history' on the grounds that it is unfair to the defendant to disallow the evidence or the question to be asked. In some cases the defence go ahead anyway, possibly using information about your past sexual and gynaecological history which may be given on the medical report.

Some judges and barristers think that by allowing a woman's past sexual history to be brought up, they are helping the case; for example, if the victim was a virgin at the time the rape took place or if she was engaged to be married, by asserting that she was 'a good girl'. But while this may help to convict some men it is more often used to get rapists off where the woman's past sexual history is greater.

The very fact that the courts still try to highlight such matters shows that prejudices are alive and just as strong in the courtroom. The idea that there is an 'ideal witness' who is sexually inexperienced, as opposed to women who have many sexual partners, thrives. In 1984 a judge said in his summing up: 'This is not one of the graver incidents. The lady was separated from her husband, so it could not be said she lost her virginity because of this matter,' and another judge in the same year gave shorter jail sentences to two rapists because he said the victims involved were prostitutes, and would 'have had sex if you had paid them.'

However the Criminal Law Revision Committee in its report to the government in 1984 on the subject of sexual offences, said of rape that it did not think complainants required any further protection during cross-examination as it could result in unfairness to defendants. It emphasized the need for judges to exclude questions which sought to establish a woman has had sexual experience in order to cast doubt on her character and recommended (as did the Scottish Law Commission) that the restriction (again at the judge's discretion) should extend to complainant's previous sexual history with the defendant. In practice it is felt that judges' nearly always decide that it is relevant, and allow it to be included.

Women Against Rape, among many others, believe judges' discretion on whether rape victims are questioned on sexual experience should be removed and the evidence should only be about what happened on that 'day' between the two people involved. A woman's private life and work are not relevant to the case. 'Ultimately we want to have a woman's sexual history made irrelevant during court proceedings. The issue is one of consent, not who the person is,' says Judit Kertesz of WAR. By eliminating such questions the treatment of rape by the courts should become much clearer. If a woman has sole rights over her body as she should, then there is only one issue and that is consent. Most women agree: in the Women's Safety Survey, carried out by WAR among women in London, ninety-one per cent thought a woman's sex life should not be brought up in court.

Without our consent

Rape is quite unique in that there are usually no witnesses to what happened, the only two people who know what really happened are the accused and you, the chief prosecution witness. In the absence of signs of struggle (particularly if the victim and offender are known to each other before the attack), or any independent evidence, it is unlikely a case will ever reach the courtroom, or if it does it will lead to an aquittal. Corroboration is looked for, (although not required in law, in practice it is almost essential for obtaining a conviction) and includes forensic evidence gathered at the medical examination, photos of injuries, clothing, and evidence of distress (for example, someone who saw you after the attack).

Very often the accused is not denying sex took place, but that the woman is lying over the fact that she had consented to intercourse. In the past there has been a tendency towards believing women are compulsive liars, particularly when it comes to rape. In 1976, Judge Sutcliffe said at the Old Bailey when summing up a rape trial: 'It is well known that women, in particular, and small boys are liable to be untruthful and invent stories.'

In theory, bruises are not necessary to secure a conviction, and judges should direct the jury that submission induced by fear is rape, but in the past it was implied that a woman need show some signs of injury to prove she physically resisted before a conviction of rape could be brought. However, the definition of rape was clarified in 1976 to stress the importance of lack of consent on the woman's part, rather than use of force by the accused. So it must be proved that the accused had sex without the woman's consent, and that she 'physically resisted, or if she did not, that her understanding and knowledge were such that she was not in a position to decide whether to consent or resist,' e.g., fear of death, in sleep, unconscious, or so young as not to understand the nature of the act.

In practice, the absence of signs of a struggle can often make it easier for the defence to claim the woman consented. Even where there is evidence, injuries do not guarantee a conviction. Zsuzsanna Adler, who researched rape trials at the Old Bailey, came across one young woman who had been locked into a room with her attacker all night and eventually got away from him by jumping out of a second floor window. She broke her hip and now has a permanent limp, the defendant was acquitted. Another witness needed several stitches for a vaginal tear, and the defence argued that such injuries were perfectly consistent with consent!

On the issue of consent, the methods employed during cross-examination can be particularly tough. You have to prove that you did not consent, the defence is out to show that you did. Questioning can follow the line of:

> You had a chain on your front door and yet when you saw him you let him in. It was three o'clock in the morning! I put it to you that you invited him into your flat because you knew what was going to happen.

or

> There was someone in the flat upstairs, yet you did not scream for help. I put it to you that you were enjoying yourself too much and that it was only when he said he had to go back to his wife that you became unhappy.

Some argue that the kind of questions put should not be allowed without some evidence to back them up. As the law stands the alleged attacker does not have to prove anything, and his 'story', however outrageous and humiliating, has to be put in the course of justice. He is innocent, until proven otherwise. It is the barrister's task to go into court and put forward defences for the alleged rapist. In theory the defence do not have to put these questions and he can if he wishes remain silent, because he does not have to prove anything. In practice the defence does cross-examine the witness but some believe there should be safeguards as to just how far they can go to allege consent.

An example was in the trial of Hutchinson in 1984: the chief prosecution witness was an eighteen-year-old who was raped in her own home with the knowledge that the rapist had already killed her mother, father and brother, who lay dead in the house. Under cross examination it was put to her that she had arranged to meet Hutchinson that night: 'I suggest that you went to your bedroom and he followed you and you put on some music. That you danced together, you kissed, you petted, you stripped off, you got on to the bed and sexual intercourse took place?' She was reduced to tears.

Such questioning is said to arouse the sympathy of the judge and jury, but it can do a lot of damage to the witness. If you are in that position, try to see it as an opportunity to deny everything your assailant is alleging. There is no point getting mad at the barrister:

he is doing his job which involves putting suggestions to you, however absurd or implausible he may think they are. Notice how the questions are phrased: 'I have to suggest to you that. . . .' which implies he may not necessarily believe what he is about to say himself, but he is compelled to put the question to you. It is not easy to stop yourself getting upset and angry at some of the things he may say. In the words of one woman:

> It takes a lot of strength to hold out during the cross-examination. But I knew he couldn't really believe what he was saying to me, it was all too outrageous: that I'd actually invited this tramp back to my flat and insisted he had sex with me! It was all a bit like a game, everyone playing the same old rules, but for the woman in the witness box it can be very painful. *Mandy.*

Although she was strong enough to withstand the cross-examination, she broke down when one of the exhibits was brought into court — a bag with the clothes she was wearing on the night of the attack, which she had to examine and identify. 'I think that was the worst moment — it brought it all back so vividly.'

Campaign groups and committees are often looking at the ways we could ease the ordeal in the courtroom, making it less distressing. Greater privacy and consideration for victims when they attend court comes high on the list.

Any recommendations have to balance the best interests of the witness against fairness to the accused. For example, it is argued that the accused or his counsel must have the right to examine or have examined witnesses against him, so it is essential the woman takes the witness box.

Many express distress at giving evidence in front of the accused. If it is essential the chief prosecution witness is seen by the jury and questioned, could not the accused be removed for this stage in proceedings and watch via a television monitor?

Imagine, too, how more frightening and distressing it must be for a child *victim* who has to go through the same procedure as an adult victim unlike juvenile *offenders* who have special courts. In incest cases, they may also be aware that what they say could lead to the break-up of the family and cases are often dropped, unless the man pleads guilty.

Particular attention has been paid to child victims in court. The only sure way to end the ordeal is not to insist they have to attend the trial (this could only be with the consent of the accused). A videotape of the child giving evidence and being questioned by both the prosecution and defence could take the place of calling the child to give evidence to a courtroom of people. Another suggestion is to screen off a section of the courtroom with one-way glass, where the judge, witness and counsel could sit together, without being able to see the accused and jury. However, this could be architecturally difficult in most British courts and it also involves a degree of deception. There is still a long way to go in looking for improvements.

The final stage

The prosecution moves to summing up, followed by the defence counsel. It is then the judge's duty to direct the jury on the law, and highlight particular aspects of the evidence before them, or facts he thinks they should consider. The judge may also warn the jury that it is dangerous to convict without corroboration, on the woman's testimony alone. This can be unfair. He must also instruct the jury that unless they are sure beyond all reasonable doubt that the accused is guilty, they must return a 'not guilty' verdict. So a man must be acquitted in cases where the jury are fairly sure he is guilty but an element of doubt is involved. This applies to any person charged with a criminal offence, not just rape.

Therefore, if a 'not guilty' verdict is given, it doesn't necessarily mean the jury did not believe you, but that they felt there was not enough evidence to remove all doubt from their minds. In Scotland there is a third possible verdict 'not proven' which can be brought in by the jury in such cases, and may be easier for the woman to come to terms with.

If a jury cannot agree the judge can accept a majority of ten to two, or order a retrial. If a 'guilty' verdict is given the accused can appeal if the original plea was 'not guilty' or he can appeal against the sentence in any case. You do not have the right to appeal if a 'not guilty' verdict is given.

When sentencing the judge considers any previous convictions which are only disclosed once the 'guilty' verdict is given.

Although the maximum penalty for rape in Britain is life imprisonment, the average penalty imposed is more often between three and five years. People argue that the sentencing often reflects on our values as a society when a bank robber can be sent down for twenty years and a rapist for two years! It invites the question: do our courts value property more than the person? A twelve-month sentence was imposed on a man who raped a seventy-year-old woman; the same sentence was imposed on a burglar for the theft of a radio cassette. Other examples of sentencing over the past ten years seem to give men licence to rape:

- Three rapists attacked a thirty-two-year old woman in her own flat where they bound and gagged, then raped, her. One was jailed for two years, the other two to twelve months' youth custody. The London Rape Crisis Centre said at the time 'This case, like so many others, illustrates how judges fail to reflect the gravity of the crime.'
- Three appeal court judges provoked a storm in 1977 when they set free a young guardsman, Tom Holdsworth, who had been jailed for three years for indecently assaulting and causing grievous bodily harm to a seventeen-year-old girl who refused to have sex with him. As a result of the attack the girl had to give up her job, and her mother had to care for her as she was partially paralysed for a time. At the trial she had been accused of having torn her own blood-stained underwear which was held up in court. It was said Holdsworth had allowed his enthusiasm for sex to overcome his normal good behaviour. When the appeal judges substituted a six month suspended sentence it was said 'The reason we have taken this course is because we don't want to see your promising army career in ruins.'
- In the summing up to a rape case in 1982 a judge referred to the expression 'Stop it, I like it,' and went on to say if a woman didn't want sexual intercourse, she had only to keep her legs shut . . . . then there would be marks if force was used. The accused was acquitted.
- A £2,000 fine was imposed on a rapist in 1982 after the judge

said there was 'contributory negligence' by the seventeen-year-old victim because she had hitched a lift. He was later rebuked by the Lord Chancellor, as 'contributory negligence' has no basis in criminal law, only in civil law.

- In December 1983 a judge gave an eighteen month sentence, suspended for two years, to a man who admitted an attempted rape, being 'vicious' towards the victim, and causing bruising to her throat. He was told by the judge, 'Off you go and don't come back to this court . . . you've never seriously been across the law before . . . for goodness sake, make this the last time. Once you put your hands around a woman's neck, when you are in drink, anything can happen.'

Following a series of 'lenient' sentences which were highlighted in the newspapers, and, in particular, one case of a man who raped a six-year-old girl and was given a year's sentence with eight months of it suspended, public outrage was such it was decided that only senior judges, authorized to try murder cases, could sit on rape trials, and that, apart from in exceptional circumstances, an immediate custodial sentence should be imposed. This was intended to restore women's faith in the courts, indicating a sterner approach to rapists.

Many believe the only real solution is to reduce the power given to judges in the first place: is too much left to their discretion — the line of questioning, directing the jury and sentencing?

For, although the proportion of convicted rapists sent to prison is high, many people believe the prison sentences imposed for rape and indecent assault are too low when compared to sentencing for other crimes. Rape can command a life sentence, but it is rarely given. Most receive sentences for less than seven years and such lenient sentences are seen to encourage rapists. Many will think they will never be caught, and even if they are what does it matter: they'll probably get away with a couple of years. As an example of this there was a case where the twenty-year-old rapist, who was found guilty with two others of raping a seventeen-year-old college student eight times, smiled and said, 'That's fair enough, thanks,' when jailed for three years.

However the idea of bringing in a statutory minimum sentence to ensure all convicted rapists are not let off too lightly at the discretion of the judge, does have its own disadvantages: women may be more reluctant to report (particularly if the man is known to them); juries may be more reluctant to convict if they think the minimim sentence is too severe for the degree of crime committed; and it could cause more rapists to turn into murderers if they think it could lead to a life sentence anyway.

The aim to get more people into the courts would be defeated.

On the other hand women would feel more secure if they knew for certain that, if convicted, their attacker would be locked away for a minimum length of time at least. For among the fears expressed by women in the Women's Safey Survey carried out by Women Against Rape, was that their attacker could be given such a short sentence that he could come back to take revenge within a few months or within a couple of years at most. An example of this was the release of James Pollard, freed on parole who went straight back to the woman he had raped two years before and whom he had threatened, 'Talk, and I'll kill you.' He carried out the threat.

In 1983 the majority of those found guilty of rape were sentenced to between two and seven years. Eighty received sentences of longer than five years, and there were only eight life sentences.

For indecent assault, only one in five (approx) received immediate prison sentences, the average being from six to eight months.

In cases of incest, almost three-quarters of those convicted received an immediate prison sentence, all but one for under five years (1982). In incest cases, the sentence imposed can be distressing on the prosecution witness too, as often she does not want to see her parent/relative sent away for a long time and may feel guilty for being the 'cause' of it.

In general, though, most women would welcome sentences which reflected the severity of the crime, so they could see justice being done, and may be more encouraged to bring their attacker to the courts.

'If you know your attacker has been jailed and you know he isn't walking about, it can help. At least there has been some justice done,' say WAR. 'There is nothing which can make the agony disappear but it is the injustice which adds to the trauma for some women. It's like the court saying, "You are wrong. This man did not rape you. You are lying."' As one young woman remarked:

> I couldn't believe it when I heard the judge saying that because the accused had served time in custody and because he was going to do community work, he was going to release him. To me that judge was saying that a man can attack you, he can threaten to kill you and leave you frightened for the rest of your life, and yet he would still be set free as long as he had a job and was not a burden on the state. Our legal system seems to have plenty of pity and compassion for the criminal, but precious little for the victim.

However, there have been encouraging signs of more sensible sentencing, and changing attitudes in the courtrooms. Once it was almost unheard of for judges to imprison men who had raped prostitutes, yet in 1984 an Old Bailey judge said 'A prostitute is as entitled to deny her consent to a man as anyone else. It goes without saying that she is as much entitled to the protection of the law if she does so.' With those words, he made public in the courtroom what women have been trying to get across for years: that a woman has sole rights to her own body. Another judgement in 1984 gave more hope for the future when a judge told the convicted rapist that however far a woman may encourage a man, if she then withdraws her consent, it is rape. 'It must be clearly understood that if a young woman indulges in kissing and cuddling and perhaps other fondling, even in these permissive days, she is entitled to say "No further".'

The move towards heavier sentencing shown in some rape cases also indicates courts are at last beginning to treat rape with the severity it deserves. It is interesting too, that there is an increase in the number of rapists being brought to trial, and this could be due partly to more women having faith in the courts because of recent cases, as well as the general increase in violent crimes as a whole. At the Old Bailey there was a record number of rape cases in one day: twelve were heard on 6 February 1985. It could indicate a frightening upward trend in the number of rapes committed, but may also show women are no longer prepared to keep their silence and want to do all they can to see rapists get what they deserve. As one woman said just two weeks after the trial:

> Even though I felt he should have been locked away for a great deal longer, I have no regrets about going into court. It was an ordeal, there is no getting away from that, but I'd say to all women go through with it. By your silence you are encouraging that man to attack again. Even if the court had found him not guilty I would have felt I'd done my bit to get him put away. Other women I've spoken to who did not report their attacker have said they felt guilt for a long time afterwards, and felt their only method of retribution had passed them by. We've got to be strong, we've got to show that even going into the witness box and being challenged is not going to stop us seeking justice.

Even when the justice is forthcoming, it doesn't stop the anger:

> He got fourteen years in all, but I still wanted to get hold of him, pin him to the floor, and slit his throat. People said I'd get it all out of my system and be able to forget once the trial was over and he'd been sent away, but I didn't and I think it's the same for a lot of women. *June 34, from Basildon.*

It can be worse when the man who attacked you is aquitted.

> I'd put a brave face on it for all those long months and now suddenly it was all over, and the full force of what had happened to me hit me for the first time. I was shattered, I felt like I'd just been raped again, victimized in the witness box. I wouldn't talk to anyone, I couldn't eat or drink, I lost a stone in weight, and on the second day after the trial ended, I blacked out.
> *Ann, from Bristol.*

There are no easy ways to come to terms with how you are feeling — if there were we would list them here. The way to recovery can be slow and painful, and it's unlikely you'll ever 'forget', but there is a road back to restoring confidence and happiness, as women in the next chapter will tell you.

7
THE LONG ROAD BACK: Life Goes On

'Of course it's changed me. I can't walk down a street alone without every nerve-end tingling and I don't trust people as I once did but I also feel more confident. Whatever happens in the future I know that I'll be able to survive.' *Pamela, from South Wales.*

'My husband has given me lots of support, too much in a way. He's there to meet me when I leave work. I don't feel I can go out alone or make any move without him: he seems to be watching me all the time. Ever since the rape I feel as though I am the one serving the sentence — and it could be for life.'

Jill, from Bristol.

'My mother died recently and I know I'll never get over that — she was the most important person in my life. The rape perhaps takes second place — it was once the most traumatic thing in my life. But life does go on, and you learn to carry these things with you as scars in the mental sense of the word: only *you* know they're there. What happened to me was horrific, but you do eventually find an inner strength to carry on.' *Cathy, 28, from London.*

The physical pain may be long healed, but the mental suffering can go on and on. Friends and family will try to encourage you to forget, to move on, they will probably not want to talk about it and will try to get you to pick up the pieces and pull yourself together. Other people's sympathy, however genuine, has a time limit. They're probably prepared to listen at first but you might find you need to talk for a long time to come:

> I still feel like talking about it now. Once I find someone who is prepared to listen I can't stop. After a few months people think you should have forgotten all about it . . . put it behind you, but every now and then I want to talk about it so much, but I feel people don't want to listen, you've had their sympathy and you can't really expect it to go on for ever.

Even those who gave you a lot of initial support may be prepared for you to be upset for a number of weeks or months but there is the notion then that you should really be getting your life back together again and they will think they are helping you to overcome it by pretending it didn't happen.

The truth is it can take years to recover — some women never get over it completely. Rape Crisis Centres are often contacted by women who were raped twenty or thirty years ago and are still suffering. It is interesting, too, that almost one in five of women who contact Rape Crisis Centres do so a year or more after the attack, probably the time when the support of friends may start to cease.

You may think you are 'over it' yourself: others urge you to forget and you try to do so but it often reappears; you can't understand why it has such a hold on you. People may even suggest you're wallowing in self pity.

> I felt so terrible because I couldn't understand why I felt so bad. I felt so devastated and no one, unless they've been through it can understand. I just couldn't slip back into normal life again as my family hoped. They stopped talking about it and because I couldn't express how I felt during the day, even with people who had given me a lot of help to begin with, I bottled it all up until night time, when I'd go to bed and think about it and keep myself awake. Part of me couldn't understand why I was making such a big thing of it two years after it had happened. Was I some kind of freak for the way I felt? *Jeanne, 26, from Bradford.*

'I think it would have helped had he been convicted,' says another woman. 'As it was I was in constant fear, and for two years afterwards I used to look for his face in crowds, and I had numerous nightmares about running up to him and shouting. Had he been caught I'm sure I'd have been more able to get on with my life.'

But even the fact that the man is convicted, doesn't signal the start of a new life. It is often the stage when those around you might push you to forget and move on. It is seen as a 'finale' in a sense, an end to all the months of misery. But as we've seen in the last chapter this is not necessarily true and it can be a very difficult time. Kay Coventry of the National Association of Victim Support Schemes explains: 'We often see how the family and friends want the woman to 'move on' after the court case. But even if the man is found guilty, it can be a very difficult patch because by that time support from friends is dwindling; they expect you to be getting on with your life, but the woman is probably still in need of lots of help and support.'

As one woman described it: 'The rapist was caught and jailed, and people said to me I should be pleased, but I'm not. He may have got five years, but I've got life. That's how I feel.'

'When a woman is raped or sexually assaulted, the effects are likely to last a long time,' says Sheffield Rape Crisis Centre. 'Don't advise a woman to "forget it" — she can't.'

Family and partners need to show great understanding and patience. A husband remembers:

> From one evening our whole lives changed. My wife's character changed, from being outgoing and independent, she was nervous and withdrawn. I took time off work to be with her at first, just to sit with her and talk. When the case eventually came to court, he was sent away for six years. I felt that was a good time to put it behind us, and think of the future, but I expected too much. It is up to the woman to say how much time she needs — it is five years now since that terrible day which still haunts her constantly. She says I cannot expect her to forget, ever, but I can help her to live with it.

Moving on

In attempting to overcome the long terms effects of rape, women can come to rely on tranquillizers, antidepressants, sleeping tablets, and/or alcohol. The suffering can get worse, not better, relationships can deteriorate and break up. Women have lost their jobs and moved home yet the nightmares and phobias continue. Unlike physical abuse, sexual abuse may leave no visible marks.

Yet the emotional scars heal far more slowly than the bruises left by physical punishment. Indeed, the effects of rape on its victims *and* their families has been found to be more severe than in the case of almost any other crime.

Because of the taboos surrounding sexuality, and the whole subject of rape, the long term sufferer is often left to go it alone. You can read about how you'll feel immediately after being raped, but little is said about how you'll feel a year or so later. Understanding these effects can help you come to terms with what is happening. It's likely that your outlook on life and the way you respond to other people can be affected by rape. Women talk of a complete personality change and being suspicious of other people:

> I've lost my spontaneity and my trust of men in general. I'm frightened driving my car alone, day or night, and I would never stop for anyone, male or female, even if it really was an accident. I'm terrified of being alone in a lift with a man and often feel as if I'm going to scream if he says anything. I feel more aggressive and angry since the rape and have suffered extreme bouts of depression. Two years afterwards I felt that if I didn't stop feeling so angry I would commit suicide. All this despite the fact that I had a loving boyfriend, who gave me all the support I could have wished for. *Kate, from London, raped six years ago.*

> It is possible to overcome the actual trauma of rape but it is difficult to come to terms with the way it changes your perspective on life. I used to be quite naive and see the best in people, now I tend to be more cynical and wary. I don't trust people as I used to — it's as though the world is a different place, much more threatening and dangerous. Perhaps this trust returns eventually but it seems to be a very long process.
>
> *Gillian, raped five years ago.*

> I didn't think friends had noticed any change in me, but some have said how I'm far less friendly and much more nervous than I used to be. I don't think I'll ever get over it completely and I think it has changed me more than I realize. I was always quite mature, but this has made me grow up so much quicker. For two years after the attack, my mum met me every night from the station after work. I

didn't go anywhere at night on my own. I went through a phase of thinking I'd never have any confidence again, for going out on my own. I know my mum has noticed the difference in me but she doesn't like to say too much. She wants me to feel I'm getting back to normal.

Mandy, from London, indecently assaulted three years ago.

It has completely changed the way I feel about people. I won't even go down the town if I think I might see someone I know. If anyone tells me I'm looking nice, I misinterpret it and I think they must be after something. I can't take people at face value. Some friends have said it's made me bitter and that I should try to see it in my heart to forgive him and show some compassion! It just shows how no-one really understands the depth of your feelings.

Pamela, from Plymouth, raped eighteen months ago.

As well as the emotional problems, there are other changes which may occur, directly resulting from the assault. Younger women have spoken about the long term effects on their education and career plans. 'My school work suffered most of all,' says one woman now in her twenties. 'I had a complete lack of concentration during my most important last year at school.' Another woman talks about the effect on her career:

I lost confidence professionally as well as in my personal life. Before this happened I had a good job as a psychologist/counsellor, but more than anything now I feel unable to get close to people.

For other women it can be the physical injury or illness rather than the mental anguish that causes them to give up their job.

Some need to move away, in particular when their house was the place of the rape, or where the attacker was known and lived locally. It can mean moving to a different town or neighbourhood, changing jobs, and losing friends in the search for security.

I tried to be rehoused. It wasn't just the terrible memories associated with the flat, but to give me the security of knowing he did not know where we lived. I had nightmares for two years, and was terrified that he would come back and rape me or my daughters. The fear wouldn't go away until we moved, and even now it is sometimes there. I don't think I'll ever feel completely safe.

Joan B., from Luton

One girl whose ordeal lasted two hours, never went back to the flat where it happened. Her family had to move all her belongings and furniture and find her another place to live.

> You never forget something like that, it stays with you forever. Even in my new place I sometimes see things like the alarm clock or a certain duvet cover which sends a cold shock through my whole body. I'm past the crying stage, but if I see anything that reminds me it serves to bring it all back.

It can cause a conflict — moving from an area you know well, surrounded by friends:

> I wish we could move away, but I'm sad too as this is an area I've grown up in and where all my friends live. But you have to get away. There are too many reminders for me around here, and as he lives in this part of London too I'm always afraid I'm going to bump into him. The only time I can forget it is when I get away completely. I went away with a friend to Ibiza and it was a complete change, and in fact I met my boyfriend out there. I'm sure I'd never have been able to get to know him if I'd been here. I felt so good when I was away, but then as soon as I came back, I was stumbling again. *Mandy, from London.*

It is inevitable there will be changes in both your personality and your life. For some women it can be a totally different way of life. In the few cases where pregnancy does result it is likely that most women would seek an abortion, but for some women their choice, or only option, is to keep the child. The reminder is with them constantly: one woman talking on a radio phone-in said she has not regretted her decision but every time she looks at her son, now nineteen, she sees the rapist.

The fact that you can't forget doesn't mean you can't restore some happiness, make new friendships and gain strength. But for this to happen you need to face up to what you've experienced. One young woman shows how she was able to do this:

> Ever since it had happened I've never really been able to talk about it. I could talk around it: I could talk about what I had felt before and how I felt when he ran off but I was too terrified to even bring myself to think about the actual rape. It was two years after the attack that I finally made myself face up to what had

> happened. I had a copy of my statement from the police and I kept it because I was determined one day I'd be able to read it through and not freeze with fear. Every time I tried to reach that point I shut it from my mind. I was convinced it would hurt too much to go through it. Eventually I reached a point in my life when everything else was going well: I had good friends and was beginning to feel happy again. I thought this is the moment I had to face up to it; if I couldn't do it now I knew I never would. I sat there and thought it all through, remembering every single thing that had happened, and then I read my statement through and realized it didn't hurt as much as I had thought.

By taking a difficult but significant step she was able to look to the future instead of being trapped in the past.

The secret past

By 'hiding' what has happened to them some women try to live a 'normal' life. Many years later it can all come flooding back: a newspaper article, a television programme, or something as seemingly insignificant as a certain smell, a fabric or a voice can bring it back as though it was yesterday. It may be another crisis in your life which forces you to remember: when things go wrong we instinctively recall all the other bad times.

The only way is to face up to it as soon as you can. When women have tried to suppress their feelings they have said the road to 'recovery' has been an uphill struggle.

> The actual date I was raped [15 May 1978] comes round as a sort of 'black' anniversary each year. You might think I had long forgotten the incident and should be living a life 'happily ever after' — not so, I'm afraid. In the course of those years I have undergone a complete character change and I'm now trying to live with the nervous, lonely isolated female I've become. I have now resorted to seeing a psychiatrist once a week, just to learn how to talk about the rape. The psychiatrist says I've suppressed all my emotions, anger, hatred and bitterness for so long, and I'm only now just beginning to talk about it and face up to the fact that the rape did happen. If only I'd let my feelings out after the rape itself, then maybe I wouldn't be suffering the way I am now, scarred for life maybe. If only I'd broken down and wept and screamed earlier on then maybe I wouldn't have had to spend so many miserable

> years and wouldn't have had three major operations (including the removal of one ovary) for pains that have since been diagnosed as 'psychosomatic'. Eventually, five years after the rape I contacted a Rape Crisis Centre. I think every woman should see a counsellor soon after it happens. Talking can help get it out of the system and with the help and support I'm getting from my psychiatrist, maybe life is going to improve. I hope so: it couldn't get worse than it has done over these bleak years, changing me into a nervous bitter recluse.
>
> Maybe one day I shall be able to accept and forget that night, but not yet. For me the nightmare still lives on.
>
> *Sylvia, from Leeds.*

Another woman talks of her 'secret' suffering:

> I can only relive that night in my mind when I'm all alone, I cannot allow myself to do so when others are around. The experience is so very personal, I cannot talk about it and there is still a definite divide between myself and others. I feel lonely and isolated, as if apart from other people, and the longer it goes on the harder it will be to ever talk about it.

Sometimes your inability to talk about the experience arises from a need to protect others, a consideration for their feelings and how it will affect them:

> I did try to talk to two of my sisters, and I desperately wanted to tell them over and over again what had happened but they found it too hard to hear. After a while, they'd say, 'Don't say anymore, I can't bear to hear it.' At first you feel angry and frustrated that they cannot even bear to *listen* to what *happened* to you. In the end I didn't want to cause them any more suffering, so I just didn't talk.
>
> *Heather, 30, from Devon*

> It is not always easy to talk, although I desperately needed to. As far as women friends were concerned I felt a need to protect them from the awful details . . . I also felt the need to protect those closest to me, especially my two daughters . . . They suffered because of the pain they saw in me and because of their lost innocence.
>
> *Joan B. from Luton.*

The result of this is that those closest to you do not know how you are suffering, yet it is your family who can be so important in your 'recovery'.

The hidden victims

When help and support is offered it is always directed at the woman who is raped, but there are many 'victims'. A whole family can be affected in different ways as a result of seeing so much pain in someone they love. A woman describes the ongoing distress caused to her parents:

> My mother and father didn't know what had happened at first. I couldn't bring myself to tell them. I delayed seeing them because I knew my mother would see a change in me, as I'd lost a lot of weight and looked very ill. When I saw her she asked questions, but I was so afraid, not for me but for her. She was not very strong, she'd had a stroke recently and I didn't want to cause further shock. But she knew something was wrong, and I had to tell her. Even though I tried to make it as painless as possible for her, without all the details, she broke down. My father was affected differently: he just told my mother not to talk about it. She was wonderful to me — she coped with my moods and my despair over the months that followed. When she died recently I was devastated, and I'm still trying to come to terms with the fact that my best friend is gone. I found out later that she had cried about it each and every day until she died.

Your family can be of enormous help but if you've never been particularly close it can widen the gap between you.

As one teenage girl still living at home says:

> I've never been close to my parents so it's hard to talk about it with them. They have tried to encourage me to tell them how I feel, but I tend to shy away. As there has always been this gap between us I find it difficult to talk about such a personal experience, and yet I have been able to talk to my brother about it. I don't think it is to do with the fact that we're close in age but more because he has always been a good friend. He's only two years older than me but he's always looked after me.

You will probably find that if you do turn to your family there may be one person who gives more support than any other.

> My mum has given me so much help, she has put a brave face on it but I know the effect that it has had on her too. It's several years ago now but I can still talk to her about it, whereas with other people they want to 'push' it away. With my nan it is one of those

> unmentionable subjects now, and with my dad — well, with him, it just didn't happen. *Wendy, 20, from London.*

Two mothers tell of the long term effects and how they've tried to help their daughters:

> It has brought us much closer, it is a secret we share. Talking about it gave her the confidence to pick up on her life again. She had come back home; said she'd left university and wanted time to rethink her life and career. At first we were angry . . . we felt she was throwing away a great chance for no reason. She became withdrawn, lost contact with her friends and resented our interference. It was only when my friend's daughter was raped abroad, that Denise blurted out the whole story that she had been raped but had told no-one, not the police or any friends. I was so shocked. I still thought of her as a child and we had never talked about sex. I just listened and hugged her. It had been a year since it happened . . . my husband just dismissed it because she would not report it to the police, but I think he could not come to terms with something so terrible happening to his daughter. She left home but writes and phones me when she needs to have someone to talk about it with, which is often.
>
> All our lives are affected: my relationship with my husband is different: it seems to have created a barrier between us, when really a crisis like this should bring a family together. While that may happen with other crises, I think rape can split a family: only women can really understand. *Jean, from Lancashire.*

> You try so hard to do what you think is best, but there is no-one to turn to or any written guidelines. Part of me wanted to get her away from where it had happened, to move to another town but then you realize that you are not really helping her face up to it. No-one can say what's right and what's wrong but I do think the best support a family can give is to encourage her to face up to it. *Betty, from London.*

Every woman needs the support and comfort from her family at this crisis time, but the extent to which it is offered depends very much on the existing family relationship: some offer nothing, some are supportive, some are over-protective. One teenage girl, an only child, had at last made the effort to leave home and move into her own flat. Soon after, she was raped and her parents insisted she move back home. They gave her all the support they could and escorted her everywhere but the effect was to reduce her to a 'child' again, completely dependent on them. It is an example of how over-protectiveness can hinder, or even prevent, recovery:

> If I'm five minutes late home my mum and dad are really frantic, and when I go to stay with friends in London they insist I ring them the minute I arrive. It's understandable but now I just want to get back to my normal routine as far as possible. I get ever so annoyed with them which isn't really fair as they only think they are doing what is right but all their questions, their over-concern, makes me feel as though I'm the one who is paying for what happened.
>
> *Michelle, from Bromley.*

The decision to 'move on', to take control of your life, will have to be yours eventually:

> I gave up work and went back to the coast to live with my boyfriend's family. They said it would be better for me as there was always someone in the house and I'd never be alone. I clung to them all in that time. I needed them for protection, to hide behind. I couldn't bear it if a stranger as much as looked at me. We got engaged and I was very docile at that time but eventually I felt I had to move away and stand on my own two feet after being so dependent on others. As I got back to my normal self I knew it wasn't right for me and I moved to a flat on my own. I felt guilty for ages though because of all that he and his family had done for me but it was time to lead my own life.
>
> *Sue, 23, from Cambridge.*

For some there are none of these problems: there is no family to be over-protective, or there is no family to which you can feel you can turn. This is particularly true of incest. You may feel an overwhelming need to protect the rest of the family from knowing what happened, or you may feel anger towards them for not being able to have done more to have prevented it. Very often the offender is someone idealized and loved by you from childhood; the immediate reaction is often great anger; long-term the feeling is one of desolation and great sadness.

Margaret is now fifty and talks of how her whole life has been directly affected by what happened to her in childhood:

> I was sexually assaulted as a child by my father and it has affected me very badly. I saw a television programme about the effects of incest, and although painful to watch, nevertheless helped me to feel better knowing that people were being informed about this crime and the way it can affect one's whole life.

Often the real impact of this crime isn't realised until you start forming relationships in your teens. Julie, who is now twenty, was sexually abused by her uncle for three years from the age of eleven until she was fourteen. It's only now she is seeing how it has affected her:

> It was when I became sixteen and had a steady relationship with my first boyfriend that realization dawned on me as to how dreadful and damaging this experience had been. I am now twenty and have just split up with my second boyfriend. We had a loving relationship but when we became physically intimate I became resentful and tense, and my boyfriend could not understand my apparent fear. I was desperately attempting to let my body, rather than my mind, take over, but the association of sexual contact with my uncle made me feel frigid and imprinted me with the idea of sex as dirty. I feel angry and shocked at my lost innocence, and to an extent emotionally damaged by the sick mind of an adult's actions of sex towards a young girl. I just feel such sadness that I felt so sexually mature and confused by the age of twelve.

Sexual abuse at a young age can destroy a girl's self-esteem: leading to a rejection of sexual maturity and a clinging to the child-like form. This can lead to something as severe as anorexia nervosa. Recent research has found that there is an important link between this disease and the incidence of child sexual abuse. Unconsciously the girl sees it as a way of warding off puberty: 'I didn't want to be attractive,' says one woman who was sexually assaulted when she was eleven. 'Initially not eating was a cry for help. I wanted someone to notice that I was unhappy but the effect of it was I became anorexic. I didn't want to be a woman, I wanted to stay a child and that seemed to make it all possible.'

Women who have been raped or sexually assaulted have similarly wanted to reject their femininity. Many have said how friends have seen them many months after the assault and have hardly recognized them because of a change in appearance: dowdy clothes, no make-up, weight change.

> I didn't want to be physically attractive and my relationship with my boyfriend provided an easy solution. He had only recently arrived in England from the Middle East and our relationship had been very casual but suddenly I threw myself completely into devoting all my time to him to save me from the horror of what had happened. For a year I bowed under to what he wanted, staying at home, giving up all my friends, even going so far as to cover myself [Islamically] which suited me fine. I wore no make-up and put on vast amounts of weight. Looking back it was a hellish sort of existence but it served its purpose.

The rejection of being a woman is much to do with warding off one of the great problems women face after rape: sexual relationships.

Sexual problems

It is not surprising, considering the nature of rape, that a main worry in restoring your life to normal is how you will overcome sexual problems. Many women fear they will be unable to form relationships with men, or where there is an existing relationship that their partner will think differently of them, perhaps no longer finding them desirable.

Your worries most likely stem from not wanting to be touched, and you fear any kind of sexual contact could cause you to relive the rape.

> It's completely affected the way I feel: I keep expecting a man who is making love to me to turn into a violent maniac. I have this fear of power and I am afraid to say 'no' to sex in case it leads to violence again.

> I married the man who was my boyfriend at the time of the rape. He has been wonderfully understanding and without him I doubt if I could ever have had a normal sexual relationship. Even now, with my husband, I still get a glimpse of that black mask — the nightmare hasn't disappeared.

If the rape is non-violent, and by someone who is known to you, people might tell you that the long-term effects will not be so serious as if you'd been brutally raped by a stranger. In fact, it is now known that it can be even more complicated, particularly with regard to forming relationships. Where the rape is not accompanied by violence, is more like 'normal sex', and involves someone you know, the effect can make all subsequent experiences of sexual intercourse 'rape-like' and destroy your trust in *all* men.

One woman's experience was able to 'prove' this theory: she was raped twice on different occasions, once by her boyfriend and then three years later by a stranger. She says it was far worse when she was raped by her boyfriend which caused her to leave college where he was also a student, give up her plans for a career and move from the area completely. The second time she was raped quite brutally at knifepoint and yet says it was less traumatic. She did not relate him to men she knew and trusted so it did not affect her ability to trust which had been quite shattered the first time.

'The result,' says Dr. Gillian Mezey of the Institute of Psychiatry, 'is that it may impinge less when it is brutal with a knife by a stranger as it is often "easier" to disassociate from the nice, caring, loving relationship you may have with your boyfriend. It's like two different things. The fact that you're having intercourse with both is somehow not relevant. When it's your boyfriend who rapes you it must destroy your ability to have satisfactory relationships thereafter.'

Jenny was raped by her boyfriend four years ago:

> I think more ought to be said about non-violent rapes and their effects, which I am sure are as traumatic as for the victims of violent rape. It doesn't mean it is easier to recover; it's rape whether it is violent or gentle and coming to terms with it takes a long, long time. I tried to behave for a long time as if nothing had happened, partly I think because it is a situation which is pretty much ignored and seen of less importance. I'd felt guilty about going to a Rape Crisis Centre as, although it was causing me a lot of personal difficulties, I felt my experience was not so important as rape with violence. Once I started talking about it all my feelings came forward: great anger, pain and destructiveness, all feelings I'd tried to suppress.'

After any kind of rape it is possible for a woman to restore good sexual relations, whether or not she is already involved in a steady relationship:

> My partner has been so gentle and caring. I know I've been lucky. Without him I would not have recovered as well as I have, and I'd never have been able to have sex with a man again. But he showed me how the rape had been torture not sexual at all, by his sensitivity and his patience. I don't make any comparison between normal sexual intercourse and rape.

And one woman who had to make new friendships says:

> Two years ago, I'd have said I don't think I'd ever be able to build up a relationship with a man, but now it's starting to become easier. I think some things are unlikely to change. Before I was raped I wanted to settle down, get married, now it doesn't bother me. But now I'm going steady with someone I met on holiday and things are starting to look brighter.

The partner involved will need to give a lot of support and understanding. He is another of the so-called 'hidden victims' and, like you, he is a victim of the myths surrounding rape and, just as you may feel confused, he will too. He can feel threatened and inadequate, he may feel offended that you associate him with the rapist or see his approaches as rape-like. However hard you both try to overcome your difficulties, it may be impossible. One man remembers sadly:

> She couldn't bear me to touch her. I was prepared for problems, and I knew it was going to be difficult, but I didn't know how severe it was going to be. It went on for months and months. How much can you take when the woman you love and want to help rejects you so completely?

Counselling may be one way you can both come to terms with the rape. Men in this situation need to understand the origins of their feelings: you may feel great anger initially at the violence used against your wife/girl friend; long-term you are more likely to feel threatened, strange as this may seem. This may be particularly so when the rapist was known to her:

> She refused to tell me who it was, it made me feel there was more to it than she was telling me. At first I tried to come to terms with

> this, but over a period of time I was unable to cope with the jealousy I was feeling, and I moved out. I still love her very much, but what happened put up such barriers between us. I still hope one day she might come to me and tell me what happened. I'm not looking to blame her but I don't feel I can help her if she doesn't tell me what happened. *John, from Sheffield*

Men may find it difficult to come to terms with not only the woman's guilt but their own. Perhaps they feel 'responsible': they were not there to pick their girlfriend up on time; they walked out after an argument. This can result in becoming over-protective: not wanting your girl friend/wife to go out alone or talk to other men. All relationships, however stable, can be torn apart by rape. A woman cannot take responsibility for her partner's feelings. He must cope with them alone which, in the past, is what he has had to do, but there is now more counselling directed towards the partners of rape victims (and also the male victims of assault). Rape Crisis Centres in a few areas, like Birmingham, Luton and Sheffield, already counsel men (in Luton they are setting up a separate counselling service for men); and the National Marriage Guidance Council will see couples (married or not) either individually or together. How a man responds to the woman's own experience is directly related to her recovery.

The amount of support and help a woman gets from friends, family and partners, as well as the kind of treatment by police are all important in coming to terms with rape. One woman says:

> If there is any woman who should recover it's me. I have had a very helpful, loving and supportive boyfriend, good friends who talked and talked with me, and also the police were very kind. They visited me at home and made sure I claimed compensation, helping me fill out the forms. I received £2,000 within six months. even though it never went to court. The money doesn't compensate for any of the pain which I still feel. But I do know I've had all the help any woman could possibly ask for, and now it's down to me. I may have beaten him physically, but now I have to beat him mentally.

For many women support does not come from family and friends, or is not the kind of help needed. In Britain there is still no automatic referral or official provision for the aftercare of women who have been raped. Instead, it comes down to how motivated and aware you are to seek help. Some women find their own way to psychotherapists, doctors or independent advice agencies. Two women talk about the lack of specialist support after such a serious and far-reaching crime:

> It took me three years to discover that I could take some kind of therapy treatment. The kind I eventually went to was feminist-orientated, which I think it needs to be. It was very helpful and I think it would help all rape victims. It should be available on the NHS, although probably in this present climate that's asking too much, but I feel it is far too important to ignore. I'm sure I would have recovered much earlier and with less suffering had I attended therapy straight away.

> A health visitor was sent to see me after the rape, but she was really out of her depth, although she did try to be reassuring. The trouble was she tried to smooth it over rather than let me express my feelings. I eventually got in touch with a marriage guidance counsellor as I couldn't afford psychotherapy at the time, and she listened to me but I didn't find it really helped. Five years after the attack, I turned to psychotherapy and only that has helped me to release a lot of anger and aggression. Through that I'm at last beginning to recover and am able to talk about it without too much pain. Just a year ago it would have been too painful. There is no Rape Crisis Centre in this area, but you need to be able to talk about your experience to someone who knows what you've been through.

It was the lack of authorized after-care and counselling of rape victims which led to the first Rape Crisis Centre being set up in Britain, in 1976 offering psychological and practical help, counselling and advice. Now they are widely spread, helping thousands of women and girls who find they have no one else to turn to. They offer confidential advice on any kind of sexual abuse, not only rape, and at any stage from immediately after a possible rape attack, to many, many years later when the initial crisis may have passed but the suffering goes on. If there is not one in your home town, contact the one nearest to you, or phone the London Rape Crisis Centre (see Resource Section).

The effects of incest can result in many problems in adult life, and here too you may find there is no-one you can turn to for advice and support. The Incest Survivors Campaign will help you: a national support and pressure network run on self-help lines, which can put you in touch with local groups where you can, if you wish, meet other women and girls who have had similar experiences, so helping one another to rebuild your strength and confidence (see Resource Section). Notice too the name of the group: the Incest *Survivors* Campaign: it will not accept the passive status implied by the term 'victim', as women who have experienced incest have often come through the hardest part and they have survived. Women will go on doing so.

Fighting back

Your recovery will be greatly aided by the help and support of other people, but it will also depend on your individual character and personality. This applies to all crises, not just rape. Women who tend to suffer more severe long term symptoms are more often those who don't have the kind of personal resources to help them cope, who have always tended to be quite anxious, or unable to show how they really feel:

> I had lots of good friends and that helped enormously to start with. But eventually it comes down to one person: you. I coped with it because I'm the kind of person who makes such a fuss about things. I think I got it right out of my system. I've never been the kind of person who bottles things up, people always know exactly what I'm feeling because I tell them! Because of that I didn't need the kind of support some people do, like Rape Crisis Centres.
>
> *Debbie, from Essex.*

Two other women describe the road to recovery as a mental battle: each day trying to overcome the experience. One day they win, the next they lose, until eventually they are able to cope with *every* day:

> I took the approach that it had happened to me, but I wasn't going to let him win by ruining the rest of my life. It was that sort of fighting attitude which I've always had: I'll show you, kind of thing. I've always been strong-willed, determined, and I'm sure that's helped me overcome this. I really do feel as though I have

> got over it: I think it would have been harder had I been physically scarred, or hadn't had the support of family and friends. But I've always loved life and going out, and this one man was not going to spoil that for me. Gradually I got to going out in the day, and then the next step was when I made a real effort and made myself go out at night. I suppose I could have quite easily gone the other way and it could have ruined my life. As it was it seemed as though I missed a year of my life. At seventeen I should have been going out to parties, with loads of friends and having a laugh. Instead I missed a whole year, and I'm not going to let him have any more of my life, it's far too valuable.

The second woman describes how it takes a certain courage to keep going when you feel at your lowest, have no outside support — because no-one knows — and make yourself face up to each day as a new challenge:

> I find each day a battle. Sometimes I win. This is when I can hold my head up high and can control my attacks of fear. Other days I lose, and the little control I have over myself is lost. I suffer from panic attacks, at least that's what I think they are, when I feel as though I can't breathe. My friends think I suffer with asthma, but I'm sure it is a result of my father when he forced himself into my mouth for the first time, and the way I gagged and felt I was suffocating. However, I feel I have suffered this far, and so can go on forever and be a stronger person for it. When I have achieved this I will then try to help others, perhaps as a teacher to recognize the special behaviour which incest victims show, and to help those who are suffering from the effects of incest as I am now.

They are encouraging words, particularly if you think you're at the stage where you'll never be able to accept what has happened to you. You probably find it hard to imagine the feeling of strength these women have found but it is possible. Not all women *do* recover, but all women *can*.

Don't rush yourself, it will take time and you will feel great depths of depression and sadness. It would be wrong to say you will come to terms with it, not all women do, and there are times when you will think it has ruined your life completely. One woman talks a year after being raped:

> I wish I could say to others that I'm coming to terms with it, getting over it, making new friendships, but I'm not. I'm very frightened of any man who tries to 'chat me up', or ask me out. I was twenty-two when I was raped and I honestly feel it has completely changed me forever. Once I was extrovert and lively, now I live in a bed-sit, don't have any sexual relationships and, despite counselling, I still can't come to terms with it. I try to 'escape', to 'switch off' and I do this by drinking too much. Generally I feel bitter and if anyone knew how I was these days they'd quite rightly accuse me of being full of self-pity. I feel very close to suicide, but unable to talk to anyone about it or seek help. I feel sorry for being so negative, but at the moment I can't forsee any happy times, new relationships, or ever forgetting what has happened.

No woman has ever said she has 'forgotten'. Rape isn't purely a physical crime. It can leave deep emotional scars. But as with other great traumas, like the death of a loved one, you eventually learn to live with it, even though you do not forget:

> I can get to sleep now without thinking about it, but it's always there as a part of me. Sometimes I hear people joking about it, and I go crazy — people just don't know enough about rape so they make out it's something to laugh at. Whenever I get like that friends think I'm getting on my soap box preaching, but I'm not going to apologize, just as I'm not going to let people laugh and joke about something so terrible. It's something I've come too close to and I don't want to forget that. It has shown a side of me I didn't know I had, and I feel stronger knowing I coped with it, and that if it should ever happen to one of my friends or family (God forbid) I'll be able to give them the support and help that you can only get from someone who has been through it.

Another woman talks five years after the rape:

> I constantly think about what has happened. It's with me every second of the day, and often at night, too, in my dreams. But gradually it impinges less and less and each day I gain strength from seeing the progress I'm making. It's changed me: I'm much more aware now. I hear the slightest noise behind me — the other day this jogger came up behind me so suddenly that I turned round and screamed. Poor guy, it's a wonder he didn't have a heart attack! But I can accept the changes, I don't think women should

> try to get back to how they were before, because that's impossible. You shouldn't see it as a sense of failure, in fact I think it can make you a much stronger person. It is such a traumatic thing to go through and get over, that if life decides to throw anything else at me, I'll know I can cope. It gives you a kind of confidence.

The strength is often gained from talking to other women, discovering that they haven't let the experience destroy them. They haven't forgotten, and it doesn't seem likely they will, but it does mean they can come to terms with it.

> I've overcome it by living in the present and the future. I try not to think about the past. I think on the whole I've made a good recovery. There aren't any sexual problems, but that's largely because of the support from my husband, and I still drive my car alone at night, although I'm more wary and apprehensive. I have helped, too, in the counselling of other rape victims and I'm hoping to become involved soon setting up a Rape Crisis Centre in my own town. Being able to offer help is, I think, the one positive thing that has come out of such an awful experience: I'm much more compassionate and caring for people and have the desire to help others who suffer. That is what I try to concentrate on, looking to the future, and this is the place from where I'm sure trust will grow again.

You may not relate exactly to the feelings of these women: you are an individual and how you come to terms with it depends on you. But you can take strength from their words, by sharing their experiences you will realize you are not alone; you are not the only person in the world it's happened to — though there are times when you think you are — and like the others you can restore confidence and happiness in your life. The past may look bleak, so concentrate on the future: a time when women will feel more able to talk about rape, like those who have done so through the pages of this book.

Women are breaking the silence. . . .

APPENDIX:
Resource Section

RECOMMENDED READING

Ask Any Woman, by Ruth E. Hall (Falling Wall Press). A London enquiry into rape and sexual assault by Women Against Rape.

The Facts of Rape, by Barbara Toner (Arrow — revised edition).

The Glasgow Rape Case, by Ross Harper and Arnot McWhinnie (Hutchinson Paperbacks).

Investigating Rape, by Ian Blair (Croom Helm). A new approach for the police.

Pictures of Women, by Jane Root (Pandora Press). A look at sexuality, myths and the law.

The Rapist Who Pays the Rent, by Ruth E. Hall, Selma James and Judit Kertesz (Falling Wall Press). Evidence submitted by Women Against Rape to the Criminal Law Revision Committee.

Sexual Violence: The Reality for Women, by the London Rape Crisis Centre (Women's Press).

Unlawful Sex, by the Howard League Working Party (Waterlow). A report on present laws, attitudes, media, victims and offenders.

Why Men Rape, by Sylvia Levine & Joseph Koenig (W H Allen).

Self-defence

Everywoman's Guide to Self Defence, by Kathleen Hudson (Collins).
Stand Your Ground, by Kaleghl Quinn (Orbis).
Teach Yourself Self Defence, by Syd Hoare (Hodder).

SPECIALIST GROUPS

For support and advice

British Pregnancy Advisory Service offers early pregnancy testing and post-coital contraception. Ring 05642 3225 for your nearest branch, or look in your local telephone book.

One Parent Families
255 Kentish Town Road
London NW5 2LX
Tel: 01-267 1361/2/3 (not Wednesdays)
(If you are pregnant as a result of rape, OPF can give advice and support if you decide to keep the child.)

Incest Survivors' Campaign
c/o South London Women's Centre
55 Acre Lane
London SW2
Tel: 01-274 7215

Also *Incest Crisis Line* Tel: 01-422 5100 or 01-890 4732

Relate: The National Marriage Guidance Council
Herbert Gray College
Little Church Street
Rugby CV21 3AP
Tel: 0788 73241

Deals with all relationship problems. Will refer you and/or your partner to local counsellors.

Women's Aid Federation

WAF offers advice and support for the victims of domestic violence. They can refer you to local women's refuges if you phone one of the following numbers:

National Helpline:	0272 428368
London:	01 251 6537
South Wales:	0222 390874
North Wales:	0970 612748
Scotland:	031 225 8011
Scottish Children's Office:	0382 24422
Northern Ireland:	0232 249041

A Woman's Place

An umbrella group for a number of women's organizations and support groups. Their address is:

Hungerford House
Embankment
London WC2
Tel: 01 836 6081

Rape Crisis Centres

Rape Crisis Centres are happy to talk to any woman or girl who has been sexually assaulted, raped, or sexually harrassed in any way. Their help is free and confidential.

BELFAST	0232 249696
BIRMINGHAM	021 233 2122
BRADFORD	0274 308270
BRIGHTON	0273 203773
CAMBRIDGE	0223 358314
CLEVELAND	0642 225787
COVENTRY	0203 77229
DUBLIN	(00) 01 601470
EDINBURGH	031 556 9437
GLASGOW	041 221 8448
LEEDS	0532 440058
LIVERPOOL	051 727 7599
LONDON	01 837 1600
LUTON	0582 33592

MANCHESTER	061 228 3602
NOTTINGHAM	0602 410440
OXFORD	0865 726295
PORTSMOUTH	0705 699511
SHEFFIELD	0742 755255
SOUTH WALES	0222 373181
STRATHCLYDE	041 221 8448
TYNESIDE	091 232 9858

Samaritans
17 Uxbridge Road
Slough SL1 3UX
(For your local group, look in your phone book.)

Taking action

Advertising Standards Authority
Brook House
2-16 Torrington Place
London WC1E 7HN
Tel: 01 580 5555

Contact them if you feel any advertising is sexist or likely to promote violence.

Child Sexual Abuse Preventative Education Project
c/o Hungerford House
Embankment
London WC2
Tel: 01 836 6081

Childline
Tel: 0800 1111

Complaints Investigation Department
New Scotland Yard
Broadway
London SW1
(If you want to complain about your treatment by the police, you should first do so to the Officer In Charge of the station.

If you are not satisfied, you may eventually have to contact the Complaints Investigation Department listed here.)

Criminal Injuries Compensation Scheme
Withington House
19-30 Alfred Place
Chenies Street
London WC1E 7LG

Safe Women's Transport
The Albany Centre
Douglas Way
London SE8
Tel: 01 692 6009

Women Against Rape
The Women's Centre
71 Tonbridge Street
London WC1
Tel: 01 837 7509

Women Against Violence Against Women
Hungerford House
Embankment
London WC2
Tel: 01 836 6081

Self defence

Stand Your Ground
49b Maldon Road
Acton
London W3 6SZ
Tel: 01 992 3021

SYG organizes self-defence courses for women, and will be able to tell you about any that are run in your area.

Contact your local police authority for details on general information on self defence in the streets.

In the same series . . .

NOW OR NEVER?

Having a Baby Later in Life

Yvonne Bostock and **Maggie Jones.** More women than ever before are having babies 'later in life' — in their thirties and even forties. Some have put off motherhood while in their twenties and put all their energies into their careers; some have married and had children early, divorced and re-married and want a second family ten to fifteen years later.

What are the problems and advantages of late motherhood? The authors deal thoroughly with all aspects of the situation, practical, emotional and medical, providing factual advice and a wealth of real-life experiences from the many women interviewed about this topic, which is of such relevance to today's woman.

THE WORKING WOMAN'S GUIDE

Women have always worked but it is only recently that the concept of a 'career woman' has become accepted. Today's working woman is rarely just filling a gap between school and marriage, but many women are still finding themselves judged in this light when it comes to matters like pay, promotion, training and even actual job opportunities. **Liz Hodgkinson** here examines the ways in which long-held attitudes mean that women are still 'second class' workers and a woman at the top of the tree something of a rarity. Here, too, is all the advice you need to make the most of every opportunity whether in career planning, interviews for jobs and promotion, combining family with career, or 'going it alone'.

THE FERTILITY AWARENESS WORKBOOK

Barbara Kass-Annese and **Dr Hal Danzer**. The Fertility Awareness Workbook does more than simply tackle the topics of reproduction and birth control – it provides every woman with the key to a greater understanding of herself and her body. Whether your particular objective is pregnancy, or the avoidance of pregnancy, this book can help. Using clearly presented diagrams and charts it shows how to recognize and record the natural monthly changes that take place within your body, so that you can identify your fertile and non-fertile times. Written in easy-to-follow 'jargon-free' language, this book is vital reading for all sexually active women.

PREMENSTRUAL SYNDROME
The Curse That Can Be Cured

Dr Caroline Shreeve. This book is for all those women whose lives are affected, every month, by symptoms which were, until very recently, termed imaginary, irrational – even insane. It is also for their families and friends, who inevitably feel the results of the premenstrual syndrome and are often as bewildered as the sufferer herself.

Caroline Shreeve is an experienced doctor, who has treated women for premenstrual syndrome for several years. She is ideally qualified to give practical and sympathetic advice on how to identify the cause of the symptoms, what to do about them, and how to cope, whether at home or at work.

THE SECOND NINE MONTHS

Judith M. Gansberg and **Arthur P. Mostel MD.** There are lots of books to advise women on coping with pregnancy and childbirth – but what about *the second nine months?* What happens to a woman *after* she gives birth?

Now you can find out what special physical and emotional reactions to expect – and how to deal with them. Everything from bringing the baby home from the hospital to going back to work.

The authors address your fears and confusions, talk about your diet, provide you with exercises to help you regain your shape, and explore the powerful issue of sex in the months following delivery. Interviews with new mothers let you know you are not alone in the way you feel.

SEX DURING PREGNANCY AND AFTER CHILDBIRTH

A Reassuring Guide for Parents-To-Be

Sylvia Close SANC. An invaluable fund of information and sound advice for young couples and a useful sourcebook for all those concerned with antenatal and postnatal care. The information is set out in an easy-to-use question and answer form and illustrated with detailed case studies. Topics include: What causes sexual apathy after childbirth? Does pregnancy affect the man or woman's interest in sex? What causes a miscarriage? Can love-making set off labour? These and many, many more questions are answered.

THE SINGLE WOMAN'S SURVIVAL GUIDE

"Marriage is traditionally the destiny offered to women by society. Most women are married, or have been, or plan to be, or suffer from not being." Simone de Beavoir. Does this statement make your blood boil? So it should! Women these days hold down good jobs and bring home high wages. They own and drive a car and very often have their own homes as well, so – if you want to be single – be proudly single. Whether you are single by design or following divorce or widowhood, this book by **Lee Rodwell** will show you how to tackle the everyday problems of life *as an individual* or, put another way, how to cope – most admirably – with being your own woman!

WOMEN ON HYSTERECTOMY

Nikki Henriques and **Anne Dickson.** Do I really NEED a hysterectomy or is there a practical alternative? How will it affect my sex life? Do they always take out the ovaries? Will I age suddenly? The authors follow the experiences of more than a dozen women who underwent the operation. They explain exactly why it is necessary, the different forms of the operation, what is actually *done*, how long it takes to get over it and how successful the operation is in actually relieving the original symptoms. It is an explicit book, but also one of hope, written for both the patient and her partner.

ALTERNATIVE HEALTH CARE FOR WOMEN

Patsy Westcott. A self-help guide to the many excellent alternative-medicine therapies especially suitable for treating women's ailments of all kinds. Divided into four sections: Staying Healthy; Women's Illnesses; Fertility and Reproduction; A-Z of Alternative Therapies — it provides practical ways for today's thinking woman to retain, or regain, her health *without* recourse to the often distressing drugs and surgery approach of orthodox medicine. *Includes advice on choosing an alternative practitioner and combining orthodox and alternative treatments.*

PREGNANCY AND CHILDBIRTH

A vital guide for the first-time-mother-to-be on the changes to expect in her own body, and the kind of assistance and options open to her through the health service. **Nicky Wesson** gives practical advice on all aspects of pregnancy, including ways in which a woman can determine what is happening to her body and her baby without the aid of professionals. She also explains various obstetric manoeuvres such as induction, episiotomy and Caesarian section together with ways of avoiding or coping with them. *Offers informed guidance to enable the right choices to be made, before, during and after the birth.*

YOUR BODY

A Woman's Guide To Her Sexual Health

Endorsed by the Marie Stopes Clinic

Designed for the 'new breed of woman' who is aware of herself as an individual, concerned about maintaining her own sexual good health and, above all, no longer content to accept a passive role in any treatment meeted out by a male-dominated medical profession. Today's woman is ready to assume responsibility for her *own* physical well-being . . . but to do this she MUST be well-informed and alert to the danger signals her body can provide. This book *gives* such vital information including: self examination; diet and exercise; infertility; sexually transmitted diseases; rape; hysterectomy; personal hygiene.

WOMAN: HER CHANGING IMAGE

A Kaleidoscope Of Five Decades

Ann Shearer looks at the changing popular image of woman in society: wife and mother; industrialist and farmer during the war years; currently freedom fighter struggling for independence; and uses the emerging pattern to project an intriguing glimpse of the woman of tomorrow that places a new perspective upon the feminist movement.